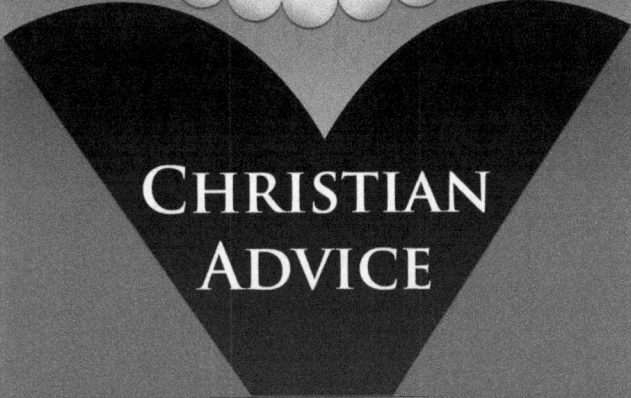

CHRISTIAN ADVICE

HUSBAND TESTED

WIFE APPROVED

FROM ONE WIFE TO ANOTHER

BY TIFFANY KAMENI

CHRISTIAN ADVICE ____FROM ONE WIFE TO ANOTHER__

TIFFANY KAMENI

ANOINTED FIRE CHRISTIAN PUBLISHING

Scriptural Verses were taken from the following Holy
Bible Translations:
King James
New International Version

PRAYER & DEDICATION

Great and wonderful FATHER in Heaven; I thank
you once again for your love, grace and mercy.
FATHER, you are my everything, and I love you
without fail. Thank you, once again, for blessing
me to write another book to bless your people.
FATHER, You are everlasting and perfect in all of
your ways.

FATHER, I ask that you let the content of this book
bless marriages on every continent. I know that you
never intended marriage to end in divorce, and I
know there is an alternative. That alternative is
called resting and trusting in You. It's not easy,
LORD, but Your people need to understand that it is
not impossible either.

FATHER, I ask that You open the eyes of Your
people as they read this book, and give them
understanding so that they may take what they have
learned and glorify you with their changed minds.
Let Your Name be glorified, perfect and wonderful
FATHER in Heaven.

In CHRIST JESUS Name I pray,
Amen.

Your daughter,
Tiffany Kameni

TESTIMONIALS

I want to personally give my review about Tiffany Kameni's New Book called Christian Advice from one wife to another. This is book was truly mind blowing in my spirit because it taught me how to become an even better wife for my husband and how to be a true help mate and how to be come an intercessor and pray for the man of God and my children and truly this book is going to help thousands of women that are wives to be encouraged on how to walk into their rightful place. This is a Best Seller! Love It!

-CHISA ROBY

After reading this work, I was forced to revisit what I actually thought about the art of COMMUNICATION. Once again Tiffany has heard the voice of God and written the needed medication for a healthy marriage from the side of the wife. So many times, relationships do not receive enough balanced feedback when it comes to conflict resolution. I think if we would give ear to the voice of reasoning through the pages of this particular work, the divorce rate would fall dramatically. It is these type of works that we miss on the main stream of information. Thank you Tiffany for this work; my prayer is that we will see one soon from the male side of the spectrum.

-PRESTON DAVIS SR.

Christian Advice From One Wife to Another is an astoundingly good book. Every wife should own a copy, and at the very least, give a copy to a good friend. It is an answer to prayer. Even though the book is from a wife's perspective, single ladies will benefit greatly from this invaluable resource; and there are certain chapters that have "words of wisdom" for men.

Indeed, this book is a treasure. One will discover that all is not lost in a dead marriage. There can be a successful resuscitation. The book is written from a Christian point of view with the validity of the Holy Scriptures taking first place as the source from which the advice emanates.

-LINDA CARDWELL

INTRO

First, let me state this: This book is NOT a woman bashing book. This book is an educational read designed to build up marriages so that the lack of knowledge can stop tearing them down.

In this book, I'm your sister who helps you to understand what you may not understand. My goal is to be that voice that says what is right and what is wrong, without being affiliated with either you or your husband. This means I'm neutral.

This book is simply an educational read put together to help the women of GOD in their marriages.

As a wife and a mentor, I have spoken with many husbands about the issues in their marriages over the course of my life and ministry. What I have found is that many of the issues that plague one man's marriage are the same issues that plague just about every man's marriage.

In this book, I will teach you more about your husband and his design. Some of the issues that arise in marriage come in because of lack of knowledge. And this lack of knowledge doesn't just come from the wife, but many men enter marriage with no knowledge of how to be a husband and an unwillingness to learn.

What we learn is that every creature has a behavior

that is characteristic of that creature. Men have certain behaviors, and women have certain behaviors. Then, add individuality on top of that, and you have a whole new breed of creature. Therefore, every man; while similar, is not the same. But when you don't know the characteristics of the creature, you can't properly care for it. You can't feed a cat dog food, and you can't place your dog in an aquarium because it's not a fish. All the same, a man of GOD has a design that has to be fueled before he can properly operate as a husband.

Knowledge is power, and in this book, you will get past the long talks and get straight to the knowledge that you need to keep peace in your marriage, keep strife away from your marriage, and keep the fire burning in your marriage.
This is about the struggles of being a wife...from a wife's point of view.

TABLE OF CONTENTS

-CHAPTER 1-

The Difference Between a Man and a Husband

"Whoso findeth a wife findeth a good thing, and obtaineth favour of the LORD" (Proverbs 18:22).

You've likely heard it said before: someone accuses a man of being a boy because of the choices he has made. Oftentimes, a man is ostracized about his choices relating to his offspring or his failures in a relationship. That's because every person has his or her own definition of what a man is and what a man is not. For example, some men would accuse other men of not being "real men" because they refuse to fight. Some women would accuse some men of not being "real men" because they refuse to sleep with them. Therefore, the definition of what a man is often differs from person to person. Nevertheless, GOD defined a man as a male being. If he was born with testicles and a penis, he is a man. If it is not a woman, it is a man. Of course, there are the rare cases in which a child is born with both the reproductive organs of a man and a woman, but this was not an accident of GOD; it was an issue of the flesh. Nevertheless, the real gender of that child can often be determined by the hormone that is most prevalent in that child. This is to say that every boy will become a man if he lives long enough.

The world's definition of a man is absolutely accurate, but many in the church have adopted the world's definition and the world's attempt to redefine a man, but the truth is: there is a difference between a man and a man of GOD. You will hear many people say that all men cheat, and they are probably right. You have to understand that the world speaks of its own; nevertheless, a man of GOD is more than just a man, and many men of GOD do not commit adultery. All the same, there is a difference between a man and a husband. Sure, a husband is a man carnally, but before he is bestowed the title of a husband, he must first become a man of GOD spiritually. If a man is not in CHRIST, yet he marries a woman, he does not become a husband; he becomes a married man. Now, in the sense of matrimony, we will still define him as a husband because a husband by our understanding is a man who married a woman. To us, he is a man; but to his wife, he is her husband.

To become a husband, a man must first become a wife to CHRIST. Now, many men probably would not embrace the title of "wife" because men are often taught to be macho in their thinking and ways. Nevertheless, the church is the bride of CHRIST. 1 Corinthians 11:3 reads, *"But I would have you know, that the head of every man is Christ; and the head of the woman is the man; and the head of Christ is God."*

Why doesn't the scripture say that a husband is the head of a wife? Why does it say that the man is head of the woman? In the Kingdom system, there are ranks. Each person of rank has a role to fill. When we don't operate according to our ranks, GOD will often demote us to protect us. 1 Timothy 2:14 sheds more light on what happened to woman as a result of Eve's choice. *"And Adam was not deceived, but the woman being deceived was in the transgression."* What we learn here is that Adam was never deceived or tricked by the enemy. He ate of the fruit, even though he knew it was wrong. His wife gave him of the fruit of the Tree of Knowledge of Good and Evil, and he ate it. He didn't ask any questions, but his choice to eat the fruit came out of rebellion. Eve's decision was made because she had been deceived. To be deceived isn't just being lied to; to be deceived means that you believed the lie. Nowhere in the Bible does it tell us that Adam believed the lie. Instead, he simply followed the lead of his wife, and this was out of order since he was created first. Because of this, GOD sent them out of the Garden of Eden and HE set up man over the woman because woman's first sin against GOD was losing her faith and desiring to be like GOD (envy). Man's first sin was to rebel against GOD for the sake of pleasing a woman. Now that the sin had been committed, envy would always be a part of a woman's struggles. All the same, women would always be unstable in their decision making because of emotions. Understand that Satan deceived Eve by triggering her emotions. You see, when Eve believed the lie, she received the lie as a part of her make-up. Her daughters, granddaughters and all women born would now bare this belief system.

Men, on the other hand, are very stable-minded and stubborn. Even if what a man believes is wrong, he will stick by it until he decides he wants to change. When a man loves and follows the LORD, he often does so with his whole heart because he's what we refer to as stubborn. He will stubbornly and wisely follow the LORD with all his might. There are men who appear to be following the LORD, but you'll discover that they are going against the very WORD of GOD in their lifestyles. Have they been deceived? No. In most cases, the issue is that the man is stubbornly following his lusts. This is an issue of his heart; or better yet, this is an issue of what he believes. He believes that his lusts will produce the fruit in which he is searching for. He still believes GOD, but he has more faith and more desire to follow his own lusts than he does the WORD. Once rebuked, a man will oftentimes make a decision as to whether he wants to repent and turn away from his lusts, or if he wants to continue after the lusts and leave the church. Again, men are stubborn creatures, and this is not an error in their design. This is actually a strength in them, because once they make up their minds to serve the LORD, it's pretty hard for the enemy to move them. That's why Satan often sends ungodly women after the men of GOD.

Women can be faithful servants as well, when their minds are made up to serve the LORD. We also know that more women go to church than men. Research says that on an average Sunday, there are generally more than 13 million more women in church than there are men. Why is this? The truth is that even though many women go to church, they still don't participate in a Christian lifestyle. Women are often moved by their emotions. For example, you will find that a large number of Christian women who frequent church are either going to church religiously (learned behavior) or because they want the promises of GOD (benefits). That's why a large number of Christian women end up having children out of wedlock or marrying a man of the world. Many women marry worldly men and then try to drag these men to church, hoping that the men will become the man of GOD that the church teaches about. Oftentimes, this behavior starts when the man is wearing the title of "boyfriend" because the woman hopes that the church will convince him to become a man of GOD and her husband.

When a man is an ungodly man frequenting church, he is often there to snare himself a woman of GOD, because he believes that she'll treat him better than a woman of the world. Ungodly men often misunderstand what the Bible teaches about Godly women. When an ungodly man hears that a woman must submit to her husband, he often believes this means he can control her. If his desire is to have power and control over a woman, he may see church as his hunting ground, especially after he has had many failed attempts at controlling women of the world. An ungodly man will learn the behaviors of believers and even learn to speak and dress like a believer. Nevertheless, he is but a mere man hoping to feed his lusts for power and control. Then again, there are some ungodly men who frequent church because they want to become Godly men. They don't know that they aren't marriage material as of yet, so they are not going to turn down a beautiful believing woman who seems to be the answer to their prayers. Women marry men who are still in transition and then get angry when they act like mere men.

But what is the difference between a man and a husband? A man is but a creature who is still under the Mosaic law; a man of GOD is a new creation in CHRIST; a husband is a man of GOD who has been led to his wife by GOD through obedience. This is done after he has accepted CHRIST into his life, of course. This means that a husband has been granted permission and access to the woman of GOD that has his rib. We are creatures of will, and we are allowed to marry whomever is willing to marry us, but a husband isn't just married; a husband is married to a wife, not a woman. Again, there is a difference. Let's read Proverbs 18:22 again. *"Whoso findeth a wife findeth a good thing, and obtaineth favour of the LORD."* The scriptures did not say whoso findeth a woman obtaineth favor; it said whoso findeth a wife. That means that GOD has already decreed that the woman in question is the help mate, other rib and life partner of the husband who found her. In her obedience, she has finally reached her season of blossoming, and she is now a wife. In the husband's season, he has finally reached his season of maturity, and he is now a husband. Please understand that a husband (by GOD'S definition) is a man who is loyal to HIM. Because he is loyal to GOD, he will be loyal to his wife. Because he trusts GOD, he will trust the wife GOD has provisioned for him. Because he listens to GOD, he will listen to his wife; he won't dominate her. Because he loves GOD with all of his heart, his heart has been enlarged to love his wife as he is commanded to love her. He won't leave nor forsake her, because he is made in the image of GOD. GOD said HE would never leave nor forsake us. If a husband after GOD'S own heart was to fall into temptation; like the Prodigal son, he would return to CHRIST because he will recognize his errors; nevertheless, a man of the world is a sinner, and the WORD tells us that a sinner will return to his sin like a dog returns to its vomit.

A husband wears the very nature of GOD. He is a protector; a provider and an encourager. He loves his wife and remains faithful to her in his attempt to remain faithful to GOD. He follows the LORD, and he stays away from any path not provided by GOD. A man strays away from the path provided by GOD to follow his own lusts. A husband has been given something sacred; something so beautiful and wonderful that GOD hid in HIMSELF, locked behind HIS will. That treasure is his wife. The husband loves the LORD so much that he is not willing to risk his relationship with GOD to commit evil against his wife. 1 Peter 3:7 reads, *"Likewise, you husbands, dwell with them according to knowledge, giving honor unto the wife, as unto the weaker vessel, and as being heirs together of the grace of life; that your prayers be not hindered."*

A husband doesn't just fear losing his wife; he fears the LORD, and because of this, he will love and honor his wife. Of course, he never wants to lose his wife; that's a given, but his love for GOD is greater than his love for his wife. This makes him a faithful man. Many women would see this as a fault in the man, because some women want the husband to love them more than GOD. This is dangerous! Any man who loves a woman more than he loves the LORD is addicted to her and could easily kill her if he felt their relationship was endangered. That's because; to him, he is her god, or she is his goddess. When a man loves the LORD with all of his heart, GOD enlarges his heart to love his wife with such a capacity that he can literally feel what she feels. When GOD calls a man a husband, and a woman a wife, and they come together in accordance to HIS will, they are favored by GOD. The Bible says that the man obtains favor, but understand that whatever the husband has trickles down to the wife.

A man serves his lusts, and he fears losing his woman. He is territorial and wears the instinct of an animal. He loves himself more than he loves the LORD; therefore, he will lord himself over his wife in an ungodly manner. A man often wants to be the king, and will not accept the Sovereignty of GOD. Sure, he will acknowledge that JEHOVAH is GOD and that JESUS CHRIST is the Son of GOD, but this means absolutely nothing to him. He will even go to church or frequent church if he feels that it will benefit him in some way. Nevertheless, his desire is to himself only. He is not faithful to GOD; therefore, it is impossible for him to be faithful to a woman. Many will try and then fail when their lusts get the best of them. A man follows the lead of the world. Whatever fad is in effect is the fad that is affecting him. As his own king, he will lead those who will follow him but follow those who lead him. He doesn't understand that his path is leading him to hell. He is more concerned about his reputation than he is about his kids or his woman. He doesn't like to frequent church; he likes to frequent gatherings where other worldly men and women are because they are either his followers or his mentors.

A man can be "in love" with you today and with another woman tomorrow. This is because he serves himself. Whatever his lust desires, he desires. You can't be angry with him; he was serving his lusts when he met you, and he was serving his lusts with you. All too often, women of GOD get with mere men and expect them to act as men of GOD. A man can put on an act for only so long before defaulting back to who he really is. He is just a man.

What you marry will determine how you live. When you marry a man, or when you marry a man of GOD who is not ordained to be your husband, you will visit and revisit trials and tribulations as you attempt to merge who you are with who he is. When you mix hot water with cold water, you'll get warm water. All the same, when you merge a woman of GOD with a man of the world, you'll get a lukewarm relationship not fit for the blessings of GOD. GOD can and will still bless the relationship if the wife remains chaste, because her husband is sanctified through her; nevertheless, she will endure some hardships that will test the depths of her faith as a result of her choice to be with him.

-CHAPTER 2-

Reflections

When you stand in front of a mirror, what do you see? You see your reflection staring back at you. You will also see everything and everyone that is behind you. When you stand in front of a mirror, the mirror will cast a reflection back to you. This reflection is the carnal you; nevertheless, a mirror can never capture the spirit of you.

As a woman of GOD, you want to be loved and adored by your husband. There is a vision in you regarding your marriage, and you'd like to see it come to pass. Right now, it may look like a far away dream that you are slowly trying to make your way towards. If the man you married is not right towards you, it's because he is not right with GOD. At this moment, he is not what you have envisioned. He likely has some good characteristics, but there are some things about him that are threatening your marriage with him. You've talked with him for a long time, and you've tried everything in your power to redirect your relationship with him. That's because women are fixers by nature. Anything that we are given, we will try to make something out of it.....even our relationships. You will find that a lot of believing women will marry unbelievers and try to make men of GOD out of them.

As a woman of GOD and a wife, there is something you should know. You are the very reflection of your husband. What does this mean? Imagine what happens when you crack a mirror. You will see the cracks in the mirror, and you will see distorted reflections of yourself between the cracks. In a cracked mirror, you can never see yourself as you are; nevertheless, many of us have had and used cracked mirrors before. We learned to work around the cracks to try to perfect ourselves. You are like a mirror. You were likely cracked by the hardships of life, or you have been shattered by something your husband did. Now when he looks at you, you are casting a reflection back at him that he does not want to see. Maybe it's a glare in your eyes or the counterfeit smile you give to him. When a man sees you, he doesn't see your hurt; he sees his reflection. This is why many men will walk away from a marriage in hopes of finding a better view of themselves. He knows and understands that the other woman is likely not his wife-to-be, but all the same, he likes what she shows him. She makes him see himself as a young and vibrant man; wanted and loved. She awakens a part of him that he thought would never live again: his lusts! The wife, on the other hand, is loved by him. She is his crown and a treasure that he will regret losing; nevertheless, he is willing to lose her to pursue this reflection that another woman is casting at him. Soon enough, he will find out that the reflection was wrong. She showed him an image that he wanted to see, but it was not the real him. He thought she would accept him as he was, and she thought she could change the way he was once he was with her. Like Eve, she was deceived to believe that she could alter who he was, and like Adam, he rebelled because she gave him the lies that Satan gave her, and he too consumed it. He knew better, but he wanted to see where the relationship would go.

As a wife, you will find that when you are angry with your husband, he will often avoid you at all costs. If he can escape to the living room, he will. If he can escape by breaking out the lawn mower and mowing the grass, he will. If he has to leave the house to escape you, he will. It's not you that he's running from; it's the reflection that you are casting. No man wants to see himself as a failure. Men tend to be prideful creatures who measure their own self-worth by the lifestyles they provide for their families. When a man is a good provider, he is more confident and will treat his wife better. When he struggles to provide for his family, he loses his confidence and will oftentimes mistreat his wife and children. It's not you (the wife) that he's mad at. Remember, you are his reflection and this is what he is yelling at. Sure, he will get mad at you because he expects you to fix the mirror that you are, so he can see himself without the cracks. Understand that you have issues too. As a wife, we tend to march around the issue yelling and hoping to see the walls come tumbling down. Of course, this would cause most men to retreat, because men not only deal with the pressures at home, but at work as well. Men tend to place a greater burden upon themselves, and they are constantly reevaluating their worth based upon how they handle that burden.

Even though the reflection is carnal, as a wife, we have to learn to cast better reflections to our husbands. First and foremost, we must be saved to be a wife; otherwise, we too are mere married women. A married woman is contentious and unstable. She is like a two-sided mirror. One day, she casts a perfect reflection to her husband, and then the next day, she will cast a shattered image that enlarges his faults and diminishes his perceived self-worth.

But what if your husband has failed at giving you the life that you want? How could you change the reflection that he sees? First, you need to understand that if the two of you are both alive, he may someday give you that lifestyle; he just hasn't reached his season yet. You also need to know and understand that sometimes the life he's giving you is a reflection of what he sees in you. A man will be different with every woman he gets with. He will still have the same flaws, but his strengths will be different because a man will often try to determine what his current woman perceives as strength. Once he picks her head and understands what she wants, he will often try to be the man she wants. For example, you can find a woman who wants nothing from life but a shack and some kids to fill it with. Let's say that her name is Judy and her husband's name is Harold. While Harold is married to her, he won't work as hard, nor will he try to provide her with nice things. With her, people may say that Harold is a bum. He may even sit at home and refuse to get a job because he can be everything she wants by being nothing but present in her life. Then again, let's say that Judy and Harold divorce, and Harold ends up marrying a woman who has a prosperous way of thinking. To everyone's surprise, Harold may get up and get a really good job or go back to school. Suddenly, he becomes a reinvented man, and he is a great provider for her. With her, he is faithful and loving, but with Judy, he was unfaithful and cruel. That's because he didn't like the reflection Judy cast back to him. Judy was a broken mirror that he got used to looking in; nevertheless, he had learned to work around her cracks for years. Now his new wife has proven herself to be a helpmate that actually helps. She doesn't necessarily have to work, but she may be an encouraging wife who supports her husband and cheers him on. She makes him feel like a man; she makes him look like the man he wants to be.

As a wife, you need to make sure that the reflection you are casting back at your husband does not hurt his feelings. Sure, some will ask, "What if he is a failure? Am I supposed to paint a picture and lie to him like it's his reflection?" No. You simply ask GOD to remove the cracks in you, and you tell him that he is beautiful no matter what he sees through you. Help him to become a better person. Remember, you are his help mate, and if you are not helping him, you are hurting him. All too often, a wife will try to dress up her husband on the outside trying to compensate what he is lacking on the inside. This actually ends up working against her because he'll then wear that outfit to see another woman who shows him a better reflection or makes him feel that she will help him to work on his image. A broken man does not want to be fixed by a woman; he wants to be encouraged as he fixes himself.

What should you do if your husband does not like the reflection he sees when he looks at you? You should encourage a change on the inside by inviting him to church, reading the Bible with him and helping him to birth out what is in him. As a wife, you will likely see his strengths and his weaknesses. Sometimes, all you have to do is start building a business or empire with the strengths you know he has and then ask him for his insights. If you build it alone, he won't participate because he'll feel like it's your project, and he doesn't want you to be the provider. But if you sit down with him and ask questions, he will feel involved. Let him think it's his idea or your idea collectively. For example, let's say that your husband's strength was relationship counseling and you've noticed this. He helps all of his friends and family members out with their relationships, and everyone seems to turn to him for advice. How could you help him? After all, he does not have a degree or a license to offer relationship counseling. This doesn't matter in the great ole states of America. It would be a great idea to start an online practice where he offers Christian counseling to couples. You would be the one who introduced the idea to him, but let him flow with his own ideas. A man has to feel like he was the author of a book before you can sell it to him. Tell him, for example, that you want to start a practice where you help Christian couples whose marriages are in trouble, but you want him to help the men. Tell him that you also want him to deal with complex questions from women about their husbands. Be sure to check the laws in your state to ensure that you can run such a practice. In most states, you can, but you have to disclose to the clients that you are not licensed and you need contracts to protect yourself. In building this online venture, you will see your husband light up as the website and company comes together. Let him hire the web designer. Let him pay for whatever he wants to pay for. As wives, we often try to relieve our husbands of the financial pressures of life, and this is crippling to and unwanted by most men. We think we are helping, but it's like cooking his favorite meal and then mixing it with something he hates. For example, it's like cooking his favorite soup and then adding okra to it when you know he hates okra. You just ruined the whole pot of soup for him!

As a help mate, your job is to be supportive of him no matter what he decides to do. Of course, if he has a bad idea that you know will work more against him than for him, you should warn him and offer a better idea. The problem with many wives is that they tear down an idea, but offer nothing in return. Men often welcome criticism when it's followed by a new idea that's worth considering. If he still wants to pursue his idea, let him. If it fails, don't wear the "I told you so" face or you'll change the way you look to him. Let him know that he has your support no matter what. In doing this, you are actually being that help mate that GOD has called you to be. Because you are doing this, he will eventually find success since he has the support of a good woman. When a husband has a good woman, he strives to do great things for her to show his appreciation to her. Always remember, a man will settle with giving you what he thinks you believe you are worth. It's not him that determines your value; it's you. He simply pays you what you are asking for.

As a wife, you should have been delivered from the souls of any men you were with before your husband. Women oftentimes bring the residue from these relationships into their marriages unknowingly. When there is residue in you from a previous relationship, you will cast the reflection of every man you've been with to your husband. This will prove to be intimidating, discouraging and hurtful to him. You don't have to say that another man is still in your heart because your words will always betray you. *"A good man out of the good treasure of his heart bringeth forth that which is good; and an evil man out of the evil treasure of his heart bringeth forth that which is evil: **for of the abundance of the heart his mouth speaketh**"* (Luke 6:45).

When another man is in your heart, you will find that your husband feels the need to constantly compete with him, or he may emotionally remove himself from the marriage. If you witness your husband competing with a man who is not in your life, just know that you are casting that man's reflection. Instead of challenging your husband, ask the LORD to deliver you from the soul tie and residue affiliated with past relationships. With soul ties, you oftentimes have to go on a fast to tear down the flesh and get to what's hiding behind the heart. A fast is like peeling a banana. You remove layers of skin to get to what's on the inside.

You are his reflection. Keep your heart clean and make sure you ask GOD to heal any hurts you have. That way, when you cast a reflection of your husband to himself, he will see himself as he is. If he is in error, he will seek to correct it. If he is doing a great job as a husband, he will be encouraged to continue.

-Chapter 3-

Ishmael or Isaac

I'm sure you've heard the story of Ishmael and
Isaac. GOD promised Abraham that HE would give
him and Sarah a son. Sarah thought she was too old
and didn't believe GOD, so she sent Abraham to
sleep with her handmaid Hagar, who was a slave
woman. Hagar conceived a son for Abraham, and
his name was Ishmael. Eventually, Sarah did
conceive a son with Abraham, and Abraham named
him Isaac. Sarah witnessed Ishmael mocking her
son one day, and she told Abraham to send Hagar
and Ishmael away. Abraham didn't want to, but
GOD told him to listen to his wife, so Abraham did.
Ishmael was a son born of the flesh, but Isaac was
the son of promise.

In relation to Christian relationships, you will often
hear people tell single women to wait for their Isaac
and stop giving in to their Ishmaels. Ishmael is
used to represent the wrong man or wrong spouse,
whereas Isaac often represents the husband of
promise. In the biblical texts, they were contrasted

in relation to the birthing of promise as opposed to works of the flesh. So it is fair to say that relationships not established in GOD by GOD were established in the flesh; therefore, worldly men who marry believing women can be symbolically referred to as Ishmael. Men of GOD who find their wives can be symbolically referred to as Isaac.

As a wife, you either have an Ishmael or an Isaac. Either your marriage partner is your GOD-sent husband, or he is a man you took in the flesh for the flesh. It's pretty easy to differentiate Isaac from Ishmael. How so? The Bible tells us that you will know a tree by the fruit it bears. What type of fruit is he bearing? Is he GOD-fearing, loving, supportive and a great provider? If so, you've likely been found by your Isaac. Is he self-serving, hateful, non-supportive and lazy? If so, you've likely got the wild man named Ishmael.

But let's say that you are now in the wilderness with Ishmael. You've married him and given children to him. Now, he is nothing but trouble for you, and he keeps shattering your dreams because he doesn't like the reflection he sees of himself when he looks at you. After all, wild men don't normally have mirrors, and when they do find one, they often break it and use it as a tool. They have no use for their reflection. What should you do? Should you cast Ishmael out or should you stay with him? First off, please understand that Ishmael was a wild man, and you can't cast a wild man out of his own forest. Why would you want to remain in the wilderness anyway? Nevertheless, the Bible tells us that you have to remain with him if he desires to stay with you. Now, that is of course if he has not committed adultery. If he is abusive towards you, of course, you can separate from him, but the Bible never said you could divorce him for abuse. Of course, abusing a woman is a very wicked and horrible thing to do; so much so that many Pastors will say to you that you can divorce your husband for this very reason. But biblically speaking, the Bible never said that abuse was a justifiable reason to GOD to file for divorce. The good news is, however, that adultery is a clause, and abusive men are often very promiscuous. 98-99.5% of abusive men commit adultery against their wives. This means that in the separation, he is likely to commit adultery, thus giving you the green light to end the marriage.

GOD hates a divorce, and HE wants you to be with your spouse through thick and thin. The Bible only speaks of three ways in which a marriage can be ended.
1. Adultery.
2. Unbeliever leaves the believer.
3. Death.

If a man is abusive towards you, it goes without saying that you need to separate yourself from him quickly. He is a dangerous man, and he is trying to get you to submit to whatever spirit is controlling him. His hunger for power and control is life-threatening, and you should not put yourself or your kids at risk trying to work things out with him. He has to change; he has to seek GOD and get delivered from his desire to be GOD in your life. An abusive man is hearing from demons; there are no ifs or buts about it. He's abusive because he wants something, and he feels that his punches or his words can force you to produce for him what he wants.

If your husband is not abusive and he has not committed adultery, you have to try to win his soul for the Kingdom. How do you do this? 1 Peter 3:1-5 reads: *"Likewise, you wives, __be in subjection__ to __your own__ husbands; that, if any obey not the word, they also may __without the word__ be won by the __conduct of the wives__; While they behold your __chaste behavior coupled with fear__. Whose adorning let it __not be that outward adorning of braiding the hair, and of wearing of gold, or of putting on of apparel__; But let it be the __hidden man__ of the heart, in that which is not corruptible, even the ornament of a __meek and quiet spirit__, which is in the sight of God of great price. For after this manner in former times the holy women also, who trusted in God, adorned themselves, being in subjection unto their own husbands..."*

There are several parts that I underlined that I would like to elaborate on.

- **Be in subjection to your own husbands.** What this means is that you have to submit to him even if he is an unbeliever. This does not mean that he gets to control you or that you follow him to hell. This means that you allow him to be the head of the house, and you allow him to make his own mistakes.

As a help mate, you would instruct him against those mistakes when you see them coming, but if he doesn't listen, let him make the mistake. Why is that? A man learns a lesson faster from his mistakes than he does from a mouthy woman. As he trips over his own pride, stumbles at his own misunderstandings and falls over bad advice, he will learn to stand on the WORD of GOD. Your job is to be there and help him back up. Your job is to love him and continue with him unless GOD tells you otherwise. Also, pay attention to the *"to your own husbands"* line. Women tend to look at another woman's husband and submit to the idea of what that man is. Many will submit to the men in their families, their bosses at work, their Pastors and their personal trainers; nevertheless, they refuse to submit to the husband. This is out of line and out of order, and it will not produce the results you want. You cannot win a soul for the Kingdom of GOD by acting like a woman of the world.

- **_"...if any obey not the word, they also may without the word be won..."_** Christian women tend to overdo it with telling their husbands about GOD but not showing their husbands that they serve the very GOD they are trying to get them to serve. Sure, you should talk to him about the LORD, but more than that, you should let him see the GOD in you. Your works will win him faster than your words.

- **Conduct of the wives.** This again applies to your works. Do you present yourself as a godly woman, or do you present yourself as the mixture of a godly woman and a worldly woman? When you behave as a woman of GOD every day, one of two things will happen: either your husband will learn to submit to CHRIST by watching you submit to HIM, or he'll abandon the marriage. That's why the WORD tells us that if the unbeliever wants to leave, let him depart. *(See 1 Corinthians 7:15)*. Why would he leave? James 4:7 explains it well. *"Submit yourselves therefore to God. Resist the devil, and he will flee from you."* When you submit to GOD, the devil and anyone submitted to the devil will move mountains trying to get away from you. Your conduct should be chaste behavior coupled by fear. Not fear of the man, but fear of GOD. The scripture also tells us that we ought to have a meek and quiet spirit. What does a meek and quiet spirit do? If you are married and you tend to be mouthy towards your husband, you will notice that he resists you or pretends to agree with you to shut you up. But what does he do when you are quiet, even though he knows that you are upset? He will likely pay more attention to you. Why is that? You leave him with his own thoughts, and you cause him to see the reflection of the person he is at that very moment. This is humbling for any man. When you fight with him, he only sees you and the reflection you are trying to show him. He'll resist that reflection, but he still won't like what he sees with you and the reflection he sees of himself in you. That's why we are called to be meek and quiet. This means let the conviction of the LORD swallow him whole.

- ***".....not be that outward adorning of braiding the hair, and of wearing of gold, or of putting on of apparel."*** In both marriages that I had, there were times when I saw the marriages going downhill. I'd tried talking; I'd tried arguing; I'd tried praying; I'd tried everything that I could think of, but to no avail. Prayer works, but the problem was that I would not submit to the men I'd married; therefore, I was not in submission to GOD unbeknownst to me. So, just like many women, I tried changing my look. I went and got my hair done beautifully, changed my clothes and even bought perfumes to make me more appealing. What I didn't know was that my attitude stunk and my ways were ugly. I was trying to dress up the outer woman, but I was doing nothing for the inner woman. The "new me" would walk through the door expecting every problem that was in the marriages to get up and run at the sight of a glamorous woman. I learned a pretty valuable lesson about men. You can be super-gorgeous and still be unappealing to a man when your attitude does not line up with your beauty. At the same time, you could be bare and looking your worst, but when you are meek and quiet, you will be the most beautiful woman he's ever seen. *(Go figure)*. As time went on, I talked to many married women and found that they'd all done the same thing. Women tend to try and fix their marriages using whatever tools we can find because we oftentimes cannot handle our overwhelming emotions. We want the problem to be fixed right away. Men oftentimes expect their wives to go in another room and fix whatever problems they have alone, because men often see the problem as the woman and her emotions. With that said, don't dress up the outer woman; work on the inner woman. Get full of wisdom, knowledge and understanding. Makeup for the soul is far better than MAC on the eyes.

- *"But let it be the <u>hidden man</u> of the heart...."* Who is the hidden man of the heart? The Bible tells us that he is not corruptible. This could only be the WORD of GOD. JESUS is the WORD of GOD. Remember in Matthew 11:29, JESUS said, *"Take my yoke upon you, and <u>learn of me</u>; <u>for I am meek</u> and <u>lowly in heart</u>: and <u>ye shall find rest</u> unto your souls."* That is to say, if you can't find rest in your house, chances are it's because you aren't being meek or lowly in heart. Let the WORD of GOD live in you and radiate through you.

If you've already wed Ishmael, you have to try to

introduce him to society, but do it slowly, or you'll embarrass yourself. As a woman, you won't be able to teach him much, since men often resist the teachings of their wives until they are much older. Just do as GOD instructed you, and you may get to see that it is possible for GOD to change your husband....even if he is a wild man!

-CHAPTER 4-

The Mind of a Man

What's funny is men have been trying to figure out how women think for years. Women are very different from men in their thinking patterns, and men are very different from women in their thinking patterns. This brings about a LOT of arguments in the home, because we often interpret one another's behaviors as misguided. The truth is we are not misguided; we are just different. GOD designed us to empower one another. You will often find that where you are strong, your husband is weak and vice versa. This isn't a reason to bash or belittle him; this is an area where you get to show yourself as a worthy help mate.

When we were little girls, we often played with our dolls and prepared ourselves to be wives. We thought of what kind of wife we'd be, what we'd say in a dispute and what kind of food we'd cook for our husbands. Men; on the other hand, prepared for war as children. We had Barbie dolls, and they had G.I. Joes. If you were raised with a brother, you have probably survived the tormenting of your Ken doll from your brother or his G.I. Joe doll. All the kissing that Barbie and Ken did was "yucky" to your brother. For this reason, Ken often lost his head. While you were somewhere watching Cinderella get swept away out of her shoes, your husband was likely somewhere watching a wrestling match.

When we became adults, we awaited our princes while men awaited their opportunities to show off their wrestling moves. Then you came along and gave him something to think about. Most men think marriage is either a long life of benefits or a long life of sorrows; there is often no in-between for men. Men who don't want to marry will often flee the scene as soon as they detect love in the air. Men who want to marry or are open for the option of marriage will oftentimes stick around to see what happens next. When they witness more smiles than frowns, they may propose to the woman they think you are. All the same, women tend to say "I do" to the men they hope their husbands will become. This means we don't often marry our spouses; we marry our ideas. For example, when my husband and I were courting one another, I would often say "okay, baby" to him whenever we were on the phone or in person. I came off as super-submissive and sweet. Needless to say, I can be sweet, but I am not a passive woman. My husband came off as strong and loving. We married our perceptions of one another, and this almost destroyed our marriage.

There are some things you, as a wife, need to know about your husband. It is vital that every wife knows about the man she has married.

1. Your husband is strong on the outside but weak on the inside. He pretends to be strong inwardly because a man fears revealing his weaknesses. As a wife, you are often weak on the outside but strong on the inside. This is why you make a great help meet for him.

2. Husbands don't usually divorce their wives; they divorce their reflections. That's why you'll find that most men who get divorced refuse to remarry; or if they do remarry, their second and third marriages often end in divorce. The problem is the new wife begins to cast a reflection to him that he's all too familiar with. In his mind, he thought the problem was the old wife, and when he recognizes the reflection of failure on his new wife, he'll abandon that union in hopes of finding a woman who can show him a better reflection. You'll often find that some men will try to settle down with worldly women. This is because she is broken, and he can see himself as he wants to see himself in her, or she may reflect his good qualities to him. If a man is having a mid-life crisis, for example, a younger (broken) woman may make him see himself as young. All the same, he gets to rescue her, and this often boosts his ego and makes him feel like a man again.

3. Men have two eyes. To them, you are either approaching them as their wife or as a warrior. When you approach a man in a contentious way, he may flash back to G.I.

Joe. While a man of GOD should not hit you, many men will contend with you with their words. As a wife, you may come to him hoping to fix whatever problems you see in the marriage. You come into the room speaking softly and lovingly, but your words woke up the warrior in him. He heard "We need to talk." Men have often learned to associate this word with combat. Instead of asking if you can talk, it is better to be soft, meek and direct with a man. He'll receive it better and the warrior in him won't wake up to defend him.

4. Gaining weight or getting older doesn't make a man lose his interest in his wife, nor will it make him commit adultery. A man often sways when he doesn't like the reflection of himself he sees in you or when he is battling a spirit of perversion.

5. Men who cheat are not always attracted to the other woman in the same way they are attracted to their spouses. Other women represent "something new" to a man. She represents the chance to feel alive again and resurrect hope that may have died in the marriage. This only makes most men sexually attracted to the other woman, but men don't oftentimes marry the other woman. Instead, they explore their own reflection in her eyes until reality sets in. You can't stop a man from committing adultery if it is in his heart; you can only lessen the chance that he will commit adultery by staying new to him and helping

him to keep hope alive.

6. When men are upset with their wives, and the wives are being mouthy, many men will often leave the house. This isn't because he wants to punish you; this is often done by a man who is searching for answers but can't think in the noise of the words being thrown at him. Remember, a meek and quiet spirit does more for the marriage than an unruly and loud spirit.

7. When a man doesn't like your female friends, it isn't always because he wants to control you; sometimes, he is trying to protect you. Yes, some men try to remove their wives' loved ones from their lives out of insecurity; nevertheless, a man of GOD will often express his disdain for a woman out of familiarity. Most men have had their fair share of women; therefore, they can be pretty discerning when it comes to women. A man can recognize a spirit of whoredom on a woman faster than another woman can recognize that spirit because he's probably had his fair share of whorish women. Women tend to look for certain behaviors, but men can often see it in the way a woman glares at them. Even more, men can often recognize envy in another woman faster than their wives can, because most men have witnessed this behavior when they were either in the world playing the field, or when other women challenged their relationships in the past. Women tend to see envy pretty clearly, but when it is on one of our friends,

we'll often ignore it in hopes that it is not pointed at us.

8. Men often see every fight as an opportunity to win or lose. Most men hate fighting; that goes without saying. But when a wife enters the room with the intent to talk or battle, she begins to look like a video game to him. That's why men will often play on words or leave you alone with your emotions. In doing this, they feel they have won the fight because they know they will never win the argument. It is always better not to fight with a man, but to talk with him. When you see the warrior waking up, retreat from the talk and approach him about the issue another way or another day. You will find that a lot of men will lovingly respond to emails, but if you verbally have that same conversation with him, he may be resistant and argumentative. Oftentimes, this is because women become emotional and men believe the war of words is about to begin.

9. Men love to be the heroes. Oftentimes, as wives, we try to do everything on our own, and this is a mistake. One act of successfully putting something together is enough to feed a man's self-worth for a week. As a wife, you must always be soft and show your husband that he is needed. Even if you know how to do everything, your husband shouldn't know this. Instead, the better way to do things is by asking him to help you with strenuous projects. I found that my husband likes the fact that I can't

reach some of the things he can reach. Even though we have a step-stool in the house, a lot of times I will call him to get something down for me just to charge him up.

10. A wife who strives to be rich by herself is setting herself up to be by herself. Always remember that marriage is a team effort. When money comes in that the husband did not earn, he'll often feel emasculated. If the money came in through a team effort, you will find that the husband seems happier and more enthusiastic about the company. But if the wife earns it, and he was not a part of the earning process, he may feel the need to contend with his wife or start an extramarital affair with a woman whom he can be the provider for. It's not bad to earn more money than your husband; it's better to help him find his niche so he can become an earner as well. Remember, you are the help mate. Some men aren't intimidated by women who earn more money, but most men are. Some say they are not intimidated by a woman who earns more money, but they often end up leaving their wives for their secretaries or the baby-sitter. They do this because they feel they can provide for those women and be the man of the house; whereas with the wife, they feel like they are less than a man. If you are building a business, encourage your husband to either build his own business or join in the business with you.

11. When a man is tapped out and

argumentative, it often means he has run out of answers. Stacking up questions and complaints will only frustrate him all the more. He needs more knowledge. Whatever area he needs more knowledge in has to be fed. Buy him a book, CD or some reading material. Whenever he is about to tap out, you need to tap in. When he is hungry, feed him.

12. Never take on the role of protector; always take on the role of nurturer. Men tend to see women as nurturing creatures, and this makes us even more appealing to them. But when the husband is in an hour of weakness, many women will try to take on the role of protector, and this is often met by sharp words from the husband. A nurturing woman supports her husband and is there for him throughout his challenges. To a lot of men, a protective woman has put on their pants and is making them wear the aprons. That's why they become volatile. Even when a man is weak, the wife has to appear soft and delicate to him. This makes him recover a lot faster because he recognizes a creature who needs protection, and he wants to make sure he holds up his end of the deal. When a woman takes on a protective role, however, a lot of men will see this as a challenge for their positions.

13. Every man has a design and a purpose. He was designed to carry out his purpose. As a wife, you need to pay attention to your husband so that you can provide him with

the proper support as he struggles to find himself or operate in his purpose. If you are not his GOD-assigned wife, you won't have the proper tools for him and vice versa. You have to know when he needs a quiet wife or when he needs a hug, a loving rebuke or a firm push.

14. Every man has a face for every situation he faces. As a wife, you must learn to recognize these faces. Of course, I'm not talking about multiple personalities; I'm talking about poker faces. Men tend to see situations as games they need to win, and they see people as characters in this game called life. You will often witness your husband change personalities when different people are around. For example, if a worldly man who likes to be intimidating approaches him, he may put his shoulders back and put on a serious face. To him, he must show that he cannot and will not be intimidated. When his boss lady is around, he may be full of jokes and compliments. When his Pastor is around, he may be humble and helpful. When your ex-boyfriend is around, his shoulders may go back again, and he may try to stake claim to you by holding your hand and being more loving towards you. When his family is around, he will often be himself. Instead of calling him out, you have to learn to respond to each face as if it was his everyday face. Sure, he may be wrong in switching personalities, but this is his perception of life

and how to play it.

What you will find is that men of GOD do still have characteristics that are similar to mere men. This is because we always need deliverance from something. As he gets more WORD in him, you will witness a change in his thinking more and more. But he can't get to a changed mind with you dragging him there; he will come on his own when he's ready to embrace a changed mind.

As a wife, your role is to serve as an usher. You usher in peace, and you usher in new knowledge. A man will often review the knowledge you're attempting to bring in and determine what's good and what is not good. Proverbs 23:7 reminds us that as a man thinks, so is he. If he thinks he is successful, he will be successful. If he thinks he is failure, he will be a failure. This is why we are called to build up our husbands. When he sees himself as a failure, it'll often reflect in and on us. When we encourage our husbands, we are telling them that we see a different reflection than what they see. We see success; we see a man after GOD'S own heart; we see a great provider and a great father. This encourages the man to continue forward and work harder, because a man is charged up when he believes his wife is proud of him.

CHAPTER 5

Role Call

I remember going through a storm with my husband. He's African, and because of his culture, he kept giving away my spot as his wife to one of his family members. This woman would contend with me for my role as the wife, and he said nothing. Instead, he kept trying to find a way to please the both of us. She not only wanted to be the wife, but she wanted to be his husband. She wanted to be in control, and I wasn't having it. No woman wants a man who is controlled by herself or another woman.

One day, I was washing the dishes, crying and praying. I wanted out of my marriage, and I was making my case to the LORD. I begin to explain to HIM the issues that were present in my marriage. I told him about how this woman was trying to push me out of my place, and how my husband saw nothing wrong with it. I told him how I felt about it, and then I heard HIS voice from within say, *"I know how you feel."* At that very moment, I was convicted. GOD was telling me that I, along with other people, of course, have often tried to take HIS place. We have challenged HIM for HIS position in our lives again and again. We have even challenged HIM for HIS position in the lives of our spouses, children and the people we hold dear to our hearts. At that moment, my tears began to dry up, and I began to repent. I knew how hurtful it was to me to have someone unlawfully challenging me for my role, and I suddenly realized that GOD deals with this everyday on a much larger scale. How does HE put up with us? Here I was asking HIM to grant me permission to divorce my husband for one person challenging me, and I know I have challenged HIM with several people. I have tried to change my husband in the past. I have tried to push my family members towards salvation. I have tried to fix my own problems when I became anxious and didn't want to wait for the seasons to play out. I have tried to play GOD, and I have failed every time.

In a relationship, everyone has his/her own position. A Godly relationship should be in the following order:
- GOD
- CHRIST
- Husband
- Wife
- Children

Many of the problems that present themselves in lives and in our marriages come as the result of someone getting out of order. We know that GOD is Sovereign; therefore, HE remains in order.

CHRIST stays in place because HE is the WORD of GOD and HE will not return to GOD void. HE accomplished what HE set out to accomplish. When someone moves, it is always someone in the flesh. Maybe the husband got out of order, or the wife forgot to submit to her husband. Maybe the children challenged one of the parents for their positions, and they were not corrected properly. Marriages almost always end when disorder takes the place of order.

Oftentimes, as a wife, I don't immediately realize when I've gotten out of order. That's because women tend to see two points: where they are and where they want to be. Men tend to see one point: where they are, and they often judge themselves from there.

When I have gotten out of order, I have stepped into my flesh and am at that time being led by my flesh. When this happens, my husband sees a distorted reflection of himself where his flaws are enlarged, and he also sees a new challenge. He often responds with a not-so-nice look that I refer to as his warning look. This look means that we are about to have a serious argument followed by him ignoring me and letting me soak in my emotions. For most women, this is pure unmerciful torment. In many cases, I think about where the conversation is headed and where I don't want it to go. Many times, I will excuse myself to another room and just pray. What I am doing is letting the LORD deal with me, rather than me dealing with my husband. Any time you have a problem with the husband and he refuses to do what is right, tell his head. His head is CHRIST JESUS. CHRIST will oftentimes put something on his mind that makes him repent of how he has been dealing with that particular situation and any other situations he may have mishandled. As a wife, our role is to let CHRIST deal with the husband's head work; we simply help with the decision-making and production.

Just as GOD does not like when we attempt to take HIS place, your husband will not like when you attempt to take on his role. Some men will verbally lash out, while others will emotionally pull back. Some men will leave the relationship altogether to reclaim their roles as men. It is always good to know who you are, what your role is, and what the borders are between who you are and who he is. In the courting process, the two of you should have discussed this, but if you didn't, it's not too late to discuss it now. Ask him what he doesn't like; especially things that you currently do. You will likely find out that you keep crossing the borders into man-country, and he may find out that he keeps crossing the border into womanhood. This is a great opportunity for the both of you to explore one another's limitations and find ways of respecting these invisible lines.

CHAPTER 6

Who Wears the Pants

I remember when I was on the dating scene, and I'd met a guy who was showing interest in me. I liked the fact that he liked to talk just like I did, but there was some confusion as to who would be the man in that relationship. He proudly boasted of his ability to cook and told me that as his wife, I would have to stay out of the kitchen. He would be the cook. There were many other things said that served as flashing lights warning me that this man was not my husband-to-be. I would never have respect for him, because I would have to wear the pants in that relationship, and he wanted to wear my pink capris. As a result, I did not enter a relationship with him, and we simply became friends.

In many marriage settings, there is often some confusion as to who will be the man of the house. When a woman has been hurt and betrayed, she will often lose her trust in men. She becomes fearful and self-reliant. She wants to be married; she wants a man she feels she can trust, but her brokenness serves as a yoke around her neck. Because of this, she may attempt to take on the role or several personalities of the head of the home. This means that she was not ready to be any man's wife since deliverance should come before marriage. But if the man has married her in her state of thinking, he now has to stand his ground for his position and refuse to back down. In doing so, either one of two things will happen: the wife will either learn to submit or she will leave the union, in which case he is free to let GOD give him the wife GOD has placed his rib in.

Woman, you are not the head of your home. I know what it's like to not trust a man. I know what it's like to fear not seeing the direction the man is taking you in. I know what it's like to watch a man fail and anxiously want to do something to get things back on track for him. I've been there; I struggle sometimes with my own feet. I want to step in when I need to step back. I want to drive when I need to simply enjoy the ride. But I had to learn my role, and I had to learn to operate in my role. You see, when you don't take your place in your marriage, you leave an "open" sign up. This opens the door for all types of demonic manifestations, because you have stepped out of order to take on a role that is not given to you by GOD.

Men are designed to get back up again when they fall. A wise man has stumbled many times, only to learn to stand on the WORD of GOD. It wasn't someone's advice that taught him to stand; it was those painful falls he endured that taught him the importance of standing. As a wife, we often try to take his role to protect him from the falls and protect ourselves from skinning our knees with him. The error in this is that he never learns to stand and begins to depend on his wife. His wife becomes his crutch, and she will undoubtedly pick up a Jezebel spirit because she is out of order and not standing under the headship or covering of her husband. Instead, she is standing on her own understanding and praying that it'll work. She then begins to emasculate her husband, because a woman cannot respect a man who submits to her. Instead, her head is uncovered, the devil comes in, and peace moves out. You will notice that in these types of relationships, the woman will begin to take on the features of a man. She appears headstrong when she's really just angry. Her countenance darkens as she begins to sit in the place of her husband. Men under the headship of a Jezebel often begin to look more feminine or behave more in a feminine way. In such relationships, you may often find that the wife works while the husband sits at home. The wife reads while the husband cooks. The wife makes all of the decisions, while the husband just follows her lead. She is wearing the pants and witchcraft is wearing her.

What should you do if your husband does not want the role of a man, and he tries to hand it to you? Hand it back to him and quick! Some men were broken by past relationships; most times, relationships with their mothers. When this happens, men often look for their mothers in their wives, and they will hand over the keys to leadership to their wives. If you take those keys, you will be out of order and in witchcraft. You simply refuse to take his spot, no matter what the cost is. Let's say that the husband wants you to work while he sits at home and takes care of the house. We can see that the men of the Bible went out and plowed the fields. The women collected water and prepared the food. This is a great example of the man being the provider and the woman taking what he provides and preparing it. This means the role of providing is for the husband. 1 Timothy 5:8 confirms this: *"But if anyone does not provide for **his** relatives, and especially for members of **his** household, **he** has denied the faith and is worse than an unbeliever" (NIV).* Therefore, if he wants to be provided for, refuse to accept his application to be your wife.

In this world today, you will find many people (even believers) who would contend with that statement and even contend with the scripture itself. As man becomes more and more distant from GOD, he sets his own rules and surrounds them with justifications. Nevertheless, the Truth shall stand. You have a role as a wife, and he has a role as your husband. Some men would literally hand you their testicles and stand by to watch you try them on if they could. These men are out of order and have subjected themselves to witchcraft.

But what if this is your husband? What if your husband is trying to take your role? It's simple; refuse to give it to him. Just sit down and do what you are supposed to do. In your position, he will find that there is no room for him. If he refuses to work, you should refuse to be the provider for him. Ask him to look under the hood of the car, even when he doesn't know what he's looking at. Ask him to take out the trash. Let him go and wash the car. Don't try to be super-woman and do these things for him because you are doing more harm than good by doing so. When he tries to be Mr. Submissive, you have to be Mrs. Even More Submissive. Don't be moved by your emotions; stay put until he gets tired of competing with you for your position. Again, he'll do one of two things: He'll either take his position as the husband, or he'll leave. If he leaves, you weren't betrayed; you were delivered. Rejoice in the LORD and wait for GOD to send your GOD-ordained husband.

What if you want to wear the pants? You've done this for so long, and everyone has gotten comfortable in their reassigned positions. Your husband submits, you lead, and the children's eyes have crossed as they try to figure out who is who. Again, it's simple; give him back his role and seek deliverance. Both of you will need to seek deliverance. Denounce witchcraft and repent. Get in your role, and refuse to walk in his role another day.

In working with ministries, I often come in contact with these types of couples. I have seen many photos where it was clear who was heading the home. From the photos alone, it is easy see the witchcraft on that family. The woman looks husky and dominant. I can see the lines on her forehead from frowning so much. I can see the lines around her mouth from yelling so much. Her face has begun to take on the features of a man's face. All the while, her husband looks feminine and barely alive. He looks meek and quiet, like he couldn't harm a fly. The dark rings around his eyes bear witness to the life being drained out of him. I've seen photos where even the children looked out of order. The boys looked like girls as they sported their lip gloss and a big woman-like smile. The girls looked boyish as they glared at the camera as if they were challenging the cameraman. This is the result of a man refusing to take his place in the home. This is a result of the wife refusing to stay in her place and letting her husband fall down in her role. If he gets in your role, you stay there and let him keep falling until he runs out of it. Your greatest weapon against the enemy is obedience to GOD.

-CHAPTER 7-

The Greatest Battle You'll Ever Lose

Satan launched a very crafty attack against the woman in the Garden of Eden. He introduced her to thinking outside of GOD. Initially, Adam and Eve simply did what GOD told them to do out of faith. They didn't consider or even know there was an alternative to serving GOD, and it's called not serving HIM. When the enemy spoke with Eve, he made her focus on herself. Genesis 3:1-6 reads: *Now the serpent was more subtle than any beast of the field which the LORD God had made. And he said unto the woman, Yea, has God said, **you** shall not eat of every tree of the garden? And the woman said unto the serpent, **We** may eat of the fruit of the trees of the garden: But of the fruit of the tree which is in the midst of the garden, God has said, **You** shall not eat of it, neither shall **you** touch it, lest **you** die. And the serpent said unto the woman, **You** shall not surely die: For God does know that in the day **you** eat thereof, then **your** eyes shall be opened, and **you** shall be as gods, knowing good and evil. And when the woman saw that the tree was good* *for food, and that it was pleasant to the eyes, and a tree to be desired to make **one** wise, she took of the fruit thereof, and did eat, and gave also unto her husband with her; and he did eat."*

When the enemy came up against Eve's mind, he introduced her to the "me" factor. He told her a lie and presented it as the truth. All the same, he attempted to dethrone GOD'S instructions by giving her an alternative. Eve had never known that there was such a thing as an alternative. He started off his attack with a question. The purpose of the question was to introduce doubt to Eve's mind. He let her answer the question, and then he introduced her to a lie mixed with some truth. Any time doubt is present, it's because lies are present. Finally, he introduced her to envy. He told her that she could be like the gods. We all know there is one true and Sovereign GOD, and HIS Name is JEHOVAH. This was the enemy's attempt to make Eve believe that there were other gods in existence, and she could become one of them. He knew that if she realized JEHOVAH was and is the only true living GOD, she would not be tempted, because this would mean clearly no other creature or spirit had ever risen up to become equal to GOD. Therefore, Satan told her she would become as one of the gods. Of course, we know the rest of the story. Adam and Eve were evicted from the Garden of Eden, and death came into mankind through them.
Nowadays, one of the biggest enemies against a marriage is selfishness. In every divorce case, you will find that one or both of the people involved were selfish; nevertheless, neither of them will

recognize their own faults.

One of the biggest issues you'll find is people who unknowingly serve themselves by serving their spouses. These are the characters who don't see their fault in the destruction of their unions, because all they remember is trying to do right by their spouses. All too often, people don't check the motives behind their own actions. If the motive for doing something good for your spouse is to get that same thing or something else in return, you are toying with creative manipulation. Everything you do ought to be done in love with no expectation. Expectation is like a mass murderer who destroys marriages in a public arena full of blind people. Of course, doing things for your spouse and expecting to get the very same respect in return seems to be reasonable thinking for most believers. But it goes against the WORD of GOD. Romans 13:8 reads, *"Owe no man any thing, but to love one another: for he that loveth another hath fulfilled the law."* To get what you want from the spouse, you must communicate what you want to the spouse. All the same, you should never do what you don't want your spouse to do, but you can't do it and expect them to follow suit. You simply stand in as an example for your spouse, but they have free will to make their own decisions and mistakes. Expectation is a yoke when it's placed on one person by another person. We are to make our communications simple, let our yes be yes and our no be no....and that's it. But when you do something for your spouse, it should be done simply because you love them and want to do it for them.

Expectation is like doing something nice for a person and then handing them a bill. This means it wasn't a blessing from a spouse to a spouse; it was a crafty attempt to manipulate the other spouse. That's why so many women and men who end up divorced don't understand that they played a hand in the dividing of their marriages. They did this by being crafty and constantly making the marriage about "me" and not "us."

Many would argue that they didn't expect or don't expect much in return, and that what they want could be easily given to them by their spouses. Men oftentimes want to watch sports without interruption. Women oftentimes want to talk about and fix present issues in a marriage. To a man, one football game a week is not too much to ask for. To a woman, one conversation a week is not too much to ask for. Nevertheless, every man and woman sees life and situations differently. The wife may want to speak to her husband on Sunday about an issue that has risen in the marriage. The husband may try to reason with her and ask her to wait until the game is over. Realizing that the games will be playing all day long, the wife becomes impatient and moody. Once the atmosphere gets too tense, the husband will often leave the house and go to a family member or friend's house to finish watching the games. What just happened here? Two selfish characters were trying to reason with one another, and of course, it didn't work. What should have happened here? The wife should know that her husband likes to watch the game on Sundays, so she should have spoken with him on Saturday or waited until Monday. The husband should have asked for the three-minute version of the problem and then offered a solution or committed to his wife that he would think about the issue and speak more on it later or during half-time. There are many solutions that can be easily applied in disagreements, but oftentimes, the individuals involved can't see past self. The wife's attitude is, "What about me? What about how I feel?" The husband's attitude is, "What about me? What about what I want?"

You can't fight "I" with "me." As a wife and a woman of GOD, you are going to always battle the selfish nature of the flesh. You should not; however, battle your husband with your flesh; you should battle your own flesh. When the enemy attacks a marriage, he doesn't launch an attack against the union itself; he launches an attack against the unity in a marriage by appealing to each spouse's selfish nature. Sometimes, you have to learn to kidnap yourself and escape to another room to deal with your flesh.

When my husband and I used to battle a lot, it was because we both had individual desires that the other was not bowing to. We stepped outside of unity and started making selfish demands at one another. We would try to hold one another's desires at ransom. We'd basically threaten to withhold something the other spouse held dear to their hearts if we weren't given what we wanted. Did Satan come in and make us fight with one another? No. All Satan had to do was entice the selfish nature of both individuals involved and watch them self-destruct.

My husband and I had an issue in our marriage that lasted for more than five years. That was almost the whole life of our marriage, and that was the meddling family member. There were times when he'd put her in her place, and then there were the times when she would slowly and quietly slither in between us. I knew this woman was battling with a Jezebel spirit, and I believe she has a Kundalini spirit, which is a serpent spirit. I knew my husband had once been Ahabed by her, and I knew he was being manipulated into believing that he owed her something, but I felt powerless to help him. All the same, I was disgusted that he was trying to submit to a woman, let alone a woman who was not his mother. I can understand a mother from time to time, but even then, a man has to stand up and be a man. For five years, I battled for my place with him. For five years, I would enjoy our seasonal vacations from her. This was the time when he'd put her in her place and she'd slither into someone else's marriage. During these times, we'd enjoy one another and live a wonderful life as husband and wife. Then, she would call him crying and he'd fall for it. After that, we would be right back at living together with no real attachment.

I was angry and I wanted a divorce. I wanted GOD to punish my husband by letting me leave him. I knew I was a great woman and wife. I knew a divorce would hurt him bitterly. I wanted him to feel what I was feeling. If you are paying attention to the last few sentences I wrote, you will see the constant use of the word "I." I'd become selfish when the attack was launched against our union. Then, one day there she was again, and the serpent's head rose up to strike our marriage...again. Quite understandably, I was tired of fighting with her. I was tired of fighting with him. I wanted my peace back, but more than that, I wanted to please GOD, so I fasted for answers.

During the fast, the LORD began to show me some things that were in me. I had to be delivered from pride. When my husband and I would argue, pride would show up and I'd start offering him a divorce. I would boast of being a good wife. I would even refer to him as my future ex-husband. I had to also be delivered from holding onto the issue between me and his family member. I'd taken my eyes off of those devils in her, and I'd placed them on her. At one point in time, I had begun to hate her, and I had to ask GOD to deliver me from that hatred. I then began to understand that the enemy didn't launch that attack against our marriage to destroy our marriage; he launched that attack with the purpose of ensnaring my husband and I with hatred and unforgiveness. He doesn't care if your marriage survives when you are broken vessels who won't bring honor to GOD. I learned that I had empowered those spirits in her by allowing them to get me to focus on my husband and how he was handling me. My focus should have been on coming against those spirits in her and that stronghold that was holding him prisoner. It wasn't until I focused on my own issues and released her to GOD that GOD moved.

Sometimes the real battle isn't against the husband; the real battle is with self, but when we are blind to the truth, we will come against our husbands instead of dealing with the issues at hand. Additionally, the angrier a spouse gets during a disagreement doesn't always reflect how intense the problem is; it reflects how hard selfishness has made their hearts.

A marriage with "me" in it is set to crumble, because "me" is a division of "us." This means the two of you are no longer standing together. Mark 3:25 reads, *"And if a house be divided against itself, that house cannot stand."* GOD speaks for unity. As a matter of truth, HE commits to being present in our unions and lives when we are unified with one another in CHRIST. *"For where two or three are gathered together in my name, there am I in the midst of them" (Mark 18:20).* Isn't it amazing that unity invites the very presence of GOD?! This is why the enemy fights marriages so fiercely. He doesn't just fight it because it is a GOD-ordained union; he fights it mostly because it is a powerful weapon against him when both parties are in submission. The husband submits to CHRIST, and the wife submits to her husband. When this happens, the enemy has no power against that union, but the couple is very powerful against him.

One of the ways he gets us to operate in self is by showing you how different you are in comparison to your spouse. He'll often remind you of how helpful and loving you've been as opposed to how selfish and inattentive your husband has been. He will often entice you into focusing on the selfishness of the husband so you can tap into your selfish nature to deal with him. For example, you may have spent $500 for your husband on his birthday. You did this because you wanted him to have a good birthday, but there was still an expectation attached to his gift. You expected him to spend $500 or more on your birthday, but when your birthday comes, he spends $25 on a sweater and promises to take you out on the weekend. At this very moment, you lose focus on "us" and start looking at what "he" didn't do for "you." That's the separation that the enemy wants.

We know that we are supposed to die to ourselves. When we don't die to self, we choose to live for self and not for GOD. This means a person who chooses their flesh has walked away from GOD to follow their own lusts. Flesh has no inheritance with GOD, and selfishness is rooted in self-worship. If we know that selfishness could come against our relationships with GOD, why don't we realize that it can be far more damaging to our personal relationships? Anytime you hear yourself saying "I" or "me," take a step back to come against the "me" character. The greatest battle you'll ever lose isn't against your spouse; it's against yourself.

Chapter 8

Fueling His Design

Understand this: You are either fueling your husband or using up his fuel. Every man of GOD has been designed by GOD for a purpose. It doesn't matter what you want to do or what he wants to do; the only way he'll find peace, joy and longevity is if he operates according to his design. It's so easy for us to get caught up in the things and mindsets of the world and begin to have the same desires and dreams as the world. But what we want isn't always what GOD wants for us. There are many people who got swallowed up by their whales and never came out because they refused to do what GOD told them to do trying to give in to their spouses. Let's face it: We are either working with GOD or against HIM in our spouse's life. That's why it is absolutely imperative for a man to seek GOD'S confirmation when he decides to court a woman. The wrong woman will always have the wrong tools in her hand. Every woman is a help meet, and she has the tools to help the man GOD ordained for her. Sure, we can get out there and marry anyone we choose to, but when we choose, we choose from the flesh.

When GOD gives our hands in marriage to a man, it's because you were designed specifically from that man's rib. Therefore, as a wife, you have tools. You have ideas, plans and strengths. You have weaknesses and shortcomings. When you stay in CHRIST and let HIM hide you in HIM, HE will begin to specifically prepare you for a particular man of GOD. HE will provide you with the tools you need to be that man's wife. If you've established soul ties along your life's journey, HE will sever them and heal you from your past hurts, and HE will do the same with your husband-to-be. When your husband is obedient, and HIS season to wear the crown of a wife is upon him, CHRIST will open the door of HIS heart and show you to him. You won't argue and bicker trying to merge yourselves together, because you will be a perfect fit for one another. Arguments will come, but they will often bear witness to one or both of you being out of order, and you will know how to repent and resubmit yourself to the order GOD has established.

But the majority of believing women won't wait that long, because GOD gave us free will. At any given moment, we are a certain age in CHRIST, and we will find ourselves attracted to men who are our age or close to our age spiritually. As women, we tend to get caught up in the clouds of our imaginations, and we end up floating into the arms of the wrong man. We often marry our imaginations and our perceptions; not the actual man who is standing at the altar. He's just a representative; a face to put onto the character who has wooed us in our dreams. We end up fighting with our spouses continually because we are in love, but not with the spouse. We have created this character all of our lives and we are in love with him. When the actual spouse came along, we put his face on our imaginary husband, and we met him at the altar. Divorce is high amongst believers because too many of us are constantly trying to get our husbands to divorce who they really are and marry our ideas of who they should be. When we say to our spouses that they have changed and we don't think we are in love with them anymore, it's not always the result of something the spouse did. Oftentimes, the issue is we have begun to accept that they are not the man we hoped they'd be; the one who'd swept us off our feet for years in our heads. And while we are standing there battling with the man we see, trying to get to the man we want, our husbands see their reflections once again. They see that they have failed to be what we want, and this is damaging to their hearts. As women, we'll keep on trying to show our spouses the benefits of being this character in our imaginations; nevertheless, men aren't emotional creatures. They are problem-solvers; therefore, most men will walk out of the door and go somewhere peaceful so they can think. How can the problem be solved? Becoming this man you so dearly want is not an option for him. He is who he is, but he tries to figure out how he can fix such a complex problem. The truth is, he can't fix it. You have to be delivered from that adulterous relationship with the man of your dreams.

Understand that GOD can and will change your

husband. All the same, GOD can and will change you. But GOD won't change your spouse or you to fit into one another's perverted idea of what a man, woman, husband or wife is. Instead, HE will constantly and methodically tear down your flesh and give you the opportunity to stop following the lead of your flesh. Once you start empowering your flesh again, HE will let it get so high (like the tower of Babel), and then make you abandon the project. Eventually, you'll get tired of having to start all over again.

Your husband's authority rests directly under CHRIST. As a man, he deals with a lot of pressures that he will not share with you because he doesn't want you to perceive him as weak or as a failure. All the same, as a believing man, he has to be constantly covered because Satan is after his life. As he builds a life for you and your children, he has certain tools that he needs. He has most of the tools, but since you are his help mate, you have some of the tools that he needs. You will often find that when you are in obedience, GOD will tell you how to instruct your husband. When he is young, he won't always listen because men tend to battle with pride, and he wants to provide the answers, not receive them from you. As he matures in CHRIST, he will discover that CHRIST is providing him with the answers through you, because pride was blocking the line for CHRIST to reach him.

Over the course of our marriage, the LORD has used me to forewarn my husband several times. Of course, he didn't always listen. There was one particular time that he still talks to this day. We had just moved back into the United States from Germany. Actually, it was his first time living in the States, even though he'd visited the States several times before. My husband had been hired at a pharmaceutical company into a training program, but it was not set to start until June. We were planning to stay with a family member of his, but because of all of the problems there, we moved in with my mother in Mississippi. While we were there, my husband wanted to learn to drive in the States and get his driver's license, so my mom and I would often take him out driving along country roads. We wanted to avoid all law enforcement because he did not have a driver's permit.

One particular day, my mom said she was going to visit my grandmother, and she would be taking my sister along with her. I was happy because I saw it as a time to be alone with my husband. Since we'd come from Germany in February, we hadn't had much alone time together. I thought about cuddling and just enjoying time together, but my husband saw it as an opportunity to perfect his driving skills since my grandmother's house was about 45 minutes away. My mom invited him to come, and he asked if he could drive. She said yes, of course, and he was thrilled. I could see that my Mom wanted him to come, but I wanted to stay at home with my husband and just enjoy peaceful alone time together. I tried to convince my husband not to go, but at first, he wouldn't listen. I began to get angry because I didn't understand why he didn't feel the way I felt. Why didn't he want to enjoy a few hours of peace and quiet with his wife? He kept smiling and answering me, but my mom was really challenging me because she saw that he wanted to go, but I was opposing him. Ordinarily, my husband would have gotten puffed up, challenged me, reminded me that he's a grown man and then left. But on this particular day, he was in a good mood, and he was laughing at the fact that I was angry. Of course, his mind was in the gutter, and he thought it was funny that I was angry, but the truth was, I just wanted to be alone with him; nothing more. He went ahead and told my mom that he would stay home, and she kept telling him that if he wanted to go, he should go; nevertheless, he stayed home. To tell you the truth, I was surprised that he stayed.

Later that day, I got a call from my sister saying that my mom had been pulled over and ticketed. That particular city she went to is pretty well-known for pulling over anyone who is not from that county. It's a very poor city, and their law enforcement is desperate. There is pretty much no such thing as a warning with them. When I told my husband what happened, he was so thankful that he had not gone. There's no way around it; had he gone, he would have been pulled over. Again, he didn't have a license, nor did he have a driver's permit; therefore, he would have likely been arrested. To this very day, he still tells people that story, and how normally he would have argued with me, but for some reason, he had a peace about it and listened to me.

This isn't to say that your husband should listen to you at all times; it is to say that GOD has given him the wisdom to know when to and when to not listen to you. Of course, there will be times when GOD tries to forewarn him through you, but your husband will be stubborn and follow through with his own plans. It will be those times when he will learn that GOD can and does speak through his wife. Trying to force him to listen is error, because you are opposing the way he was designed. A man was designed to lead his wife but follow CHRIST. A wise man knows to pay attention to what his wife says; keep the meat and throw away the bones. A prideful man, on the other hand, will not listen because he's still trying to prove himself worthy of the title of "man." It's not your job to humble him; your job is to remain chaste and try not to laugh when he stumbles over himself.

Every man has his own unique design, but there are some characteristics that you will find in just about every man alive. These characteristics are not necessarily a part of his character; some are a part of his build, and some are perversions often found in men. Here are a few things that you, as a wife or soon-to-be wife, should know about your husband:

1. Envy is strongest in the woman, but pride is strongest in the man. Men tend to battle pride because of misguided teachings of what and who a man is. When you battle a man who is puffed up with pride, you'll lose the battle because you are arguing with air. The best thing to do is remain meek and humble so he'll feel the conviction of the

HOLY GHOST and humble himself.

2. Trying to be the provider for a man will always prove to be disastrous. Men can find themselves attracted to women who are willing to provide for them but are usually more attracted to women whom they can provide for. Just as women tend to lose respect for dependent men; men tend to lose interest in women who are too independent. It's not always that they are intimidated by such women; it's just that they don't feel they can be the "man" with her, and they fear ending up with her last name.

3. Men are natural tillers of the ground, or workers. When a man loses his job, he often goes into depression and becomes moody because he can't provide for his family. This makes him feel worthless and as if he was a burden to his family. Instead of trying to show him that you can handle all of the bills alone, the best thing to do is just let him do what he does best: try to figure it out until he realizes he needs GOD. You can conduct searches online (unbeknownst to him) to see who's hiring in your area. If you find someone that's hiring, you can casually mention it to him without telling him that you searched out this info.

4. Men often hate to argue because they don't find their strength in their words; they find their strength in their hands. If he's a man of GOD, he knows not to put his hands on you in the wrong way; nevertheless, women tend to be the boss of words. Because he loses

this battle, a man will excuse himself to go somewhere and think about the problem he sees; not the one you say. Men are thinkers, and it is better to tell them what is wrong and leave them alone so they can think about it. Doing this will often produce a better and faster result than arguing.

5. Men hate problems; they prefer solutions. I used to blabber on and on about what was wrong in my marriage to my husband. That was until he discovered how to end my forty-minute rants. When I would start talking, he'd let me get about five minutes into my rant and then cut me off. He would ask me, "Okay. What is the solution you propose?" Of course, this would confuse me, because I had this long speech prepared in my mind that I wanted to get out. I realized during those conversations that I had no solution to propose. It taught me to come to him only when I had a solution and not when I had a problem.

6. Women see talking as the solution to a problem; men see sex as the conclusion of a problem. You want to talk about it; he wants to make up and make out. It's not because he doesn't want to fix the problem; he just wants more time to think about it, but he doesn't want to have a problem with you.

7. You've got two to five minutes to make your point before a man signs out of the conversation, and the count-down begins the minute you say, "We need to talk." Women are like lawyers; we like to build our cases

against our husbands, so we'll talk for hours about a single problem. Men are like judges; they want you to get straight to the point, and then they require a recess before they come back with a decision.

8. Men are hunters by nature. Even when you get married, he has to continue hunting you and what he wants to remain interested. If you make everything easy for him, he will lose interest, and sometimes he won't know why he's lost interest. It's okay to request a date every weekend; it's okay to say no to whatever he is requesting sometimes. You know how crippling it is to give a child everything they want without requiring they work for it, right? It's the same thing with men. Even though you love seeing him happy, you need to understand that he is happiest when he's hunting. Think about how a cat is. You can have a cat living in your house, and feed him more than enough food, but if a mouse was to run by him, he'd still stalk and kill it. Why is that? After all, he's not hungry. It's because his instinct is to hunt, and that can never be removed from him.

9. Men are designed to earn. Anything they didn't earn, they won't respect.

10. When a man feels he knows everything about you; he'll often feel that he knows nothing about you. It's not because he thinks you are hiding something; it is often because he wants to believe you are hiding something. That way, he can go hunting. As

a wife, you have to continue to grow with wisdom, knowledge and understanding. Just when your husband thought he knew you, he should find out something new and fascinating about you. This keeps him hunting, and it keeps his interest.

As I mentioned earlier, every man is unique to himself. The traits above are common to men; nevertheless, you have to learn the unique character of your husband. To fuel his design, you must know his Designer, JESUS CHRIST. Otherwise, you'll end up trying to use the wrong fuel on him and getting hurt when the relationship is not working. Be that supportive and meek wife that he needs, and don't forget to be quiet. What's funny is, I can remember in both times that I was married, I received the most compliments when I was quiet; sometimes asleep. To this very day, I can always warm my husband's heart by simply looking at him and smiling. That alone is enough to win any argument.

-CHAPTER 9-

An Unworthy Trade-In

One of the issues we often find ourselves faced with
is the reality that our spouses are not perfect. The
average woman can handle that part, but the part
that we have trouble with is understanding that our
husbands are not the "men of our dreams." They
are their own men uniquely formed to be who they
are. They can be both handsome and unflattering at
the same time. They are not always there when we
need them, but GOD is. They are not always as
sensitive as we want them to be in our emotional
hour. They may not look like that chiseled man on
the television set, but we have learned to forgive
them for that. They may not earn that six or seven-
figure income that our imaginary husbands were
earning. They may not be as sharp as a nail, but
they can be as dull as a butter knife. They aren't
perfect, and that's our reality! But guess what?
They aren't perfect on purpose!

There is a reason our husbands aren't everything we
need plus some. The reason is we would find no
use for GOD if everything we needed was wrapped

up in a man. Our relationships with our spouses were designed by GOD to help us better understand and build our relationships with HIM. How imperfect we are to GOD and our spouses?! Nevertheless, being loved as the imperfect creatures that we are is a blessing in itself. Hollywood didn't just attack your husband by showing you this perfect, sensitive and loving man who repented to his wife by singing beautiful lullabies. Hollywood also threw some pretty big swords at you by showing your husband this beautiful, perfectly curved woman who woke up wearing make-up and a smile. Yet and still, you can rest assured that you are loved; even when you aren't likable.

Love is pretty amazing, but there are so many women who trade men that love them for men who lust after them. You see, a man who loves you won't always say the right things, do the right things or be there when you need him. He'll try to do all of the above, but his imperfections always catch up with him. A man who lusts after you, on the other hand, doesn't mind saying what you want to hear, doing what you need to be done, and being there for you when you need him. But understand his goal is himself, not you. A man who lusts after you can buy you the world and still not think the world of you. Everything he does is for his own ego boost. When he sends you roses on your job, it's not because he loves you; it is because he wants to appeal to you and your co-workers. It feels good to watch a bunch of naïve women stand around and melt at such a cheap gesture. A man who loves you will do more than that. Women need to hear this, because so many women trade off being married for a bouquet of roses and a high feeling that is scheduled to become bitterness.

A woman I once knew had a really good husband. He was taking care of children who were not his own, and he loved the LORD with all his heart. He worked hard to provide for her and the children she'd came in with; nevertheless, one day she began to have an affair. She wouldn't tell me about the affair initially, because she knew I would rebuke her. I overhead her speaking, and this is how I found out.

One day, she came to me and told me that she was divorcing her husband, and I asked her for her reason. She began to list all of the imperfections that he had and things he had done to her over the years. In all of her speaking, I didn't hear one thing he'd done that merited a divorce. I knew what the real reason was. Another man had become one with her, and he was appealing to her imagination. He started coming off as the "man of her dreams," whereas she knew the reality of who her husband was. She wanted to trade something real for something imagined. Of course, I tried to talk her out of it and told her how good her husband was to her, but she wasn't hearing it. The soul tie was there, and her husband was now the monster who was trying to keep her away from happiness. That's what Satan tells adulterers. I wanted to spank her with a hot skillet when she told me that her husband was begging her to worship the LORD with him. You see, I was going through a divorce from a man, and my dream had been for him to come to CHRIST. My dream was that we could worship the LORD together. But here she was....she had what so many women wanted, and she was throwing it away for a feeling. There was nothing I could do for her. Her mind was made up, and she filed for divorce.

Needless to say, she ended up getting that divorce, and the other man didn't waste any time tossing her out like a used napkin. I shook my head as I watched her re-enter the game of dating when she once had the coveted position of a wife and traded it off to be a girlfriend. That's like giving up your position as a queen to be a peasant's concubine. Over the years, I have seen this happen many times, and it never ends well.

When you are married, there will be a lot of men you will find attractive. If Satan can get you to dream about and eventually believe that one of these men is or can be better than your husband, he will come after you full force. Satan knows what you like; after all, he's the one who planted that mess in you. If your heart isn't guarded, Satan will send a man your way one day who appears to be everything that you want and need. He'll look like an angel because Satan does masquerade himself as an angel of light. *(See 2 Corinthians 7:14).* He will say the right things and do the right things. If you want a man in the church, Satan will send you a hypocrite. If you want the man to speak a certain way, he will fake his way into your heart. The sound of his voice will send shivers throughout your body, and the touch of his hand will make you weak. He will appear to be manlier than your husband. As a matter of fact, he will come off as being protective of you, even wanting to protect you from the "bad man" you've told him about. It's all a show, however. That man has only as much power as you have given him. He appeals to that little girl in you, the one who believes in fairy tales and happy endings without the work.

What about your husband? Suddenly, he will look weak and disgusting to you. Every wrong thing about him will suddenly be magnified. You'll notice that tooth that seems to be yellowing in his mouth. You'll notice that blackhead behind his ear that seems to mock you when he passes by. You'll notice that bad breath he has sometimes; the very same bad breath that didn't bother you when you were "in love" with him. When he makes a mistake, you'll magnify it a hundred times. Because of what you now believe, his kisses will become disgusting to you. Lovemaking will be so horrid that you'll look for ways to avoid being with him. The touch of his hand will become so repulsive that you'll push him away any time he tries to embrace you. After a while, you may even find yourself hating him because he is now your enemy; the man who dares to think he's going to keep you away from being happy. This is the mind of an adulteress, and it is a dangerous way of thinking.

If you don't repent and stop carrying on with that other man, you will get the rude awakening of a lifetime. You'll get that divorce you want, and you may even snag that man you think you want. Once you get in the house with him, however, he'll change from being the man of your dreams to becoming the man of your nightmares. He won't trust you because he knows how he got you. He'll try to drive everyone who loves you away from your life because he fears what the truth will do to you. After all, he's been filling you with lies, and he can't have someone come along and place doubt in you. He's worked too hard to get you, and now he doesn't want to lose you. But is it love that makes him act this way? No. He's demon-filled and power-addicted. You fed his lusts, and anytime you feed something, it will grow. He's not obsessed with you, as the world would have you to believe. He's obsessed with those imaginations that Satan gave him. Satan told him that he could be in control of the beautiful and anointed you. Satan told him that you were like his Mommy, but he could control the woman in you by preventing you from going anywhere. Satan told him that you need to be beaten when you think about going outside of his commands. After hitting you, he became aroused, because the power he felt throwing each blow at you has made him want to lay down with you. He felt loved because you received those licks and you're still there. To him, this is love, because he does not know GOD.

Suddenly, your mind will go back to the husband you once had, and you'll realize that he was a great man and husband. You'll now wish you had popped that blackhead behind his ear. You'll wish you had taken him to the dentist to find out what was going on with that yellowed tooth. You'll realize how much you miss the smell of him and his bad breath. He will now become the man you dream about as your nightmare unfolds.

This is the reality of so many women who loved a lie so much that they divorced the truth to marry it. Your husband was not and is not perfect. GOD refers to HIMSELF as our husbands, and we know HE is perfect. GOD wanted you to continue to worship HIM while with your imperfect husband. GOD wanted you to depend on HIM and not your husband. When your husband was failing, GOD wanted you to turn to HIM so HE could iron out your husband's path. That's why HE called you a help meet. But instead of turning to HIM, you turned on HIM because you allowed "me" to get in your way. Your love for GOD has to be so great that it runs over into your marriage. Your fear of GOD has to be so great that you won't come against your husband because you understand that it is the same as coming against his head; CHRIST JESUS. Your faith in GOD has to be so solid that you believe GOD can take an imperfect man and an imperfect woman and create a perfect love in HIM that surpasses the hands of time.

There is no man worth trading your husband in for. Instead, try and understand that marriage is forgiveness training. To have a forgiving heart is to have a heart like GOD. HE forgave you for your wrongs; HE doesn't lose interest in you because of your imperfections (and they are many); he doesn't mistreat you when he sees another woman of GOD behaving better than you. HE loves you still. If you desire to be like HIM, you must start practicing in your own home, with your own husband.

Chapter 10

Recovering From Adultery

In every marriage book I write, I have to speak on this subject, because adultery destroys more marriages than any other offense, save pride. Adultery is outright betrayal, and it cuts the betrayed spouse so deep that it often takes years to heal from.

One of the hardest seasons to endure for a spouse is one in which they are recovering from the reckless acts of their significant other. It is a season where adultery has ripped through a marriage and left the union in ruins. I think what makes the recovery so difficult is indecisiveness. The offended party often battles with deciding whether to leave or stay. The offending party often wants to distance him or herself from the act as far as he or she can so everything can return to normal. People don't like to be the guilty parties in any situation; therefore, the offending party may often act defensive because they are already dealing with the guilt of what they did; they don't want to deal with the conversations or the ridicule.

I tell people all the time (and I've heard it said) that adultery feels just like the death of a spouse. First, there is the period in which the spouse is committing adultery. This period is like watching your marriage die and not being able to do anything about it. You try to speak life into the marriage. You try to pray about it. You've cried and you've tried to talk about it, but everything seems for nothing. The worst part is knowing that the person who was once your best friend is now treating you like an enemy. The person you'd once fallen so hard for is no longer there. The person walking around is a familiar shell on the outside, but you don't recognize who they have become on the inside. If the marriage ends because of the adultery, the divorce proceedings are like watching the person you love being lowered into the ground. All you can do is pick up the pieces of your life and try to make a new life with it, all the while mourning the loss of the person you loved.

Along with the act of adultery, one of the worst things the offending spouse can do is be insensitive towards the spouse they've betrayed. Oftentimes, when a person is insensitive, it's because they haven't truly repented of what they've done. This means they haven't ended the affair, they are likely to restart the affair, or they will likely initiate an affair with someone else. In order for a spouse to truly repent of what they've done, they have to be broken. Sometimes seeing that they've hurt someone they love is enough to break them, while others are more stubborn and must endure an even greater fall before they'll see the error in their ways. Remember, you can't break them; it takes the hand of GOD to make a man truly repent.

Your Spouse Committed Adultery

There aren't enough words to comfort a person who's been broken by adultery, and I mean that in the literal sense. If your husband committed adultery against you, you have likely asked him a thousand questions. You want to know why he did it, where his conscience was, when he did it and why he didn't stop. Your "inner voice" is active, and you know you couldn't cheat on him; nevertheless, it's confusing and hurting that he could do it to you. But there is something you need to know as a wife. He doesn't have the words that will heal you. The only thing the husband can give you to help you get through the healing process is the whole truth. When you ask questions, they shouldn't be questions that only cement his guilt; the questions should only be to remove the lies he told you.

As a woman, I understand that you were hurt, and you are searching for anything to heal you. You think a hug will do it; you think another confession will do it; you think watching your husband suffer will do it, but none of those things work. There are three things you need to recover from an affair, and they are:

- The WORD of GOD
- The Truth Without the Details
- Time

It goes without saying that if you are trying to recover, you have decided to stay, and I commend you for this. I have spoken with a lot of women who were dealing with affairs, and most of them were being encouraged to leave their marriages by other Christian leaders. Many of them were comforted when I told them that it was okay to stay with the man if they so choose. The issue with most folks is that they tell you to move based on how they feel. Should you stay? That's totally up to you, but understand that staying means that you have to process what happened and put it behind you. You can't keep bringing it back up, and you can't make present and future decisions based on his past decisions.

To get the healing you need, I would recommend that you write him a note. Make the note short and to the point. In the note, simply lay out the issue, your point of action and an offer to close the matter. You see, most men won't speak on the affair if they think you're going to bring it up again and again.

The note could read like this:
Dear Baby,
I'm sorry that I have been distant lately. I love you and I know that you love me. Baby, I need you in this hour of my life. I know we've talked about it before, but I want to get this issue out of our marriage once and for all, so I'm proposing a marriage meeting. I would like to invite you to speak with your loving wife later today. Please see the following details:

Invitation to Restart Our Marriage
Theme: A Love That Lasts Always
When: Today, September 11th 2013
Where: In Our Bedroom
Time: 8:00pm-10:00pm
Speaker: You
Guest Speaker: Your Loving Wife
Details: I would like to speak with you concerning our marriage and what we can do to move forward from here. I do have some unanswered questions, but I am committing to you that after tonight, we will put this behind us. I will try not to be emotional, and I won't get angry with you regardless of what comes forward. The purpose of this meeting is to initiate a new start, because I really miss smiling with you.
Special Requests: No anger, no lies and no negative emotions. We are going to make this meeting a loving one where we aren't discussing the problem as much as we are discussing the solution.
Refreshments: We'll see. (Add Happy Face Here)

In this note, you will see that:
- I am trying to work with his design and not against it.
- I spoke solutions because husbands often hate problems, but they are open to solutions.
- I wrote this as an invitation so that he won't feel as if I'm trying to force him into a conversation that he likely does not want to have.
- I wrote that I needed him because men have "hero syndrome", and they often like to save

their wives, but they won't enter a conversation they think may turn out to be an ambush.

- I apologized for my distance because I was accepting responsibility for a wrong I'd committed. In doing this, I was letting him know that the meeting is not going to be me lynching him; it'll be a discussion of how to get past where we are.

- I offered a closing for the issue, because men oftentimes won't sign a deal that they can't close.

- I listed him as the speaker. If he thinks he's coming to a nagging session, he'll make an excuse or just go ahead and hurt your feelings by refusing to come to the meeting. If he knows that you are planning to listen to him, he's likely to show up to see how it all goes.

- I gave a start time and an end time, because if a man fears that you'll be talking all night long, he's definitely going to be a no-show. He may attempt to change the time from 8-10 to 8-9 or 8-8:30. Be open for negotiations or he may clam up.

- Notice that my theme is "A Love That Lasts Always." The theme is there to let him know that I plan to continue the marriage with him, and that the meeting isn't one where we'll end up talking about divorce and who gets what in the event of a divorce.

- Finally, I made mention that "refreshments" may be served. You're grown; you know what the refreshments are. But I was letting him know that the meeting is set to end on a positive note. He's likely to come to that meeting prepared to tell all and bare all...depending on how you are.

You must be willing to end the feud and move forward from there. No, it's not easy, but just ask him to hold you when you're feeling down. Let him know that there will be times when the pain will resurface, but tell him that you are trying to heal. Some men fear that you'll end up using the affair as leverage against them. Let him see that this is not your intention. When you are feeling the pain from it, excuse yourself to another room and begin to minister to yourself. Pray, cry, read your Bible...do whatever you need to do, but don't mistreat your husband. Please know that you cannot punish him; you can only place him in GOD'S hands if you really want him to be changed and if you want to continue in the marriage.

One of the biggest obstacles to being healed is the infamous "why." If a husband cheats on his wife, his wife is likely going to want to know his reason for doing so. When she doesn't get the reason, she oftentimes won't go through the door of healing because there are still some questions there she wants answered. Why did he cheat? No one can answer specifically for your husband, but here are a few reasons as to why some men cheat. (Notice I didn't say all men, because all men do not cheat).
1. **Selfishness**- All affairs are rooted in selfishness, no matter how you twist it up or bend it.

2. **The Thrill of the Hunt**- Let's face it; men are hunters by nature, BUT when a man's heart is perverted, he begins to hunt in the wrong direction. Perverted means to turn away from GOD'S original plan.

3. **Bad Association**- A lot of men are pressured to be their friends' definition of what a man is and what a man does. Bad association aka peer pressure will always ruin a man. Men often challenge one another by daring each other, and this oftentimes serves as a snare to the man's soul and his marriage. Sometimes, men try to carry on friendly relationships with other women, thinking that the friendship is harmless. This opens the door for an affair, because if his she-friend decides that she wants to start an affair with him, she has access to him to tempt him. Women can be extremely crafty and seductive. One minute, they'll pretend to be the man's friend; the next minute, they'll come on to them. I have heard countless stories from men about women using this pattern: Start a friendship, pretend to like the wife, act hurt and surprised that the wife is not reciprocating, call the married man crying about what their man did to them, call the married man crying about the alleged break-up, called the man asking him to come by and help with something, and then they snare them once they get in their houses.

4. **Curiosity**- Some men are one-time cheaters. They'll cheat out of curiosity, and then the

guilt would be too intense for them to repeat the act. Always remember and remind your family to cast down all evil imagination and every high thing that exalts itself against the knowledge of GOD.

5. **To Restore Their Self-Worth**- Some men feel worthless at home, but they feel like kings elsewhere. His self-worth could have been attacked by something you said or did, or it could have been challenged by the fact that he wasn't providing for his family. That's why men who don't have jobs are more likely to commit adultery than men who do work. At home, in his wife's eyes, he sees a reflection of failure; even though she doesn't purposely try to give it off. His conscience may be riddling him with guilt every time he sees his spouse. But with the other woman, he can pretend to be everything he isn't with you.

6. **Addiction to Sex**- This is purely demonic, and he has to be delivered. Oftentimes, it isn't the sex he's addicted to; it's the power he feels with her. Or it could be that he's turned on by forbidden fruit. Either way, it's perversion and the cure is for him to turn his heart back to GOD in its entirety.

7. **Pornography**- Men who like pornography are FAR more likely to commit adultery than men who don't. Porn opens doors in the demonic that allow all manners of flesh demons to enter.

8. **Revenge**- Some men commit adultery to take revenge against their wives for

something they (the wives) have done, or
something they believe their wives have
done.
Whatever his reason is, forgive him. If you stay
with him, forgive him; if you leave him, forgive
him. Either way, you have to forgive him and move
on. No one can make you live in misery; you have
to choose to take control of your own thoughts and
move on.

You Committed Adultery Against Him

If you have committed adultery against him, you
need to understand how your betrayal has torn him
down in order to help him in his restoration. Men
have a harder time recovering from adultery than
women do. It doesn't hurt them more than it hurts
us; it just impacts them in a different way.
Remember that mirror we discussed earlier? Well,
with men, you are that mirror, and every choice you
make reflects to them whether they are a failure or a
success. If you have committed adultery against
them, they see so many words on that mirror. They
see failure, less than a man, punk, sissy and so on.
At one point, they were your tower; a castle you
could go to for safety, but now they feel dwarfed by
the presence of another man. To a man, your choice
to commit adultery signifies that he is not enough of
a man for you; therefore, they don't just deal with
the hurt; they deal with self perception, anger and
humiliation. Don't get me wrong; women deal with
these as well, but society tends to be forgiving to a
man who commits adultery, and his wife is often not
shunned for staying with him. Nevertheless, when a

wife commits adultery against her husband, society expects him to leave her. If he does not, his image is tarnished forever. This is the very society that he depends on to provide for his family and to cultivate an image for himself. Understand that men hurt too; they just don't show it as well as we do. Oftentimes, when that hurt from the affair resurfaces in a man, he won't show you that he's in pain; he'll instead show anger or a stone face. Men would rather leave the house and deal with their pain somewhere alone than to show their vulnerable side to a woman who has betrayed them.

What should you do to recover your marriage? Here are a few tips:

1. **Accept Responsibility for Your Actions-** If you did it, say you did it, and don't try to share the fault of it with your husband.

2. **Understand That He is in Pain-** He needs time to heal, and this can often take years to come. Be understanding, loyal and supportive. The worst thing you can do is try to rush his healing.

3. **Tell the Whole Truth-** Just like women, men tend to ask questions when their wives have committed adultery against them. I know it's uncomfortable to sit there and talk about what you did, but it's better to tell him the whole truth now than it is to let him keep finding things out on his own. If he knows the whole truth, he can start the healing process. If he knows bits and pieces of the story, he can't fully heal, because the truth will keep coming out piece by piece.

Sometimes, it takes years for the whole truth to come out. This means that the marriage ends up suffering for years because the wife decided to hold back as much as she can. Be careful, however. You know your husband. If you think it could be dangerous telling him the whole truth, then be quiet. Don't lie.

4. **Ask Yourself Why You Did It**- Everything that lives has a root. Why did you commit adultery? You need to ask yourself and GOD this so that you won't return to the sin. All the same, you'll be able to offer a sound answer to your husband when he questions you.

5. **Don't Overcompensate For It**- When you carry around guilt, you'll try to buy your way out of it. This is error, because anything you do or give to him out of guilt is a reminder to him what you have done. It's hard for him to get back to normal with you, when all he sees is a guilty woman trying to overcompensate for what she has done. Just be there for him, and be supportive.

6. **Remove All Reminders**- There are many things that will remind him of what you have done. For example, that outfit you wore to see the other man must be destroyed. That hairdo you wore is now off limits. All clothing, furniture and anything you used while committing adultery should be destroyed. If you used your car to see the other man, you should really consider looking for a new car....maybe trading it in.

You don't want triggers lying around your home.

7. **Return to Normal**- The worst part of an affair is the foreign feeling that comes on both parties. Suddenly, he realizes that he doesn't know you like he thought he knew you. Suddenly, he doesn't know what normal is anymore. The longer he is in this state of mind, the more likely he is to abandon the marriage. You need to return your household back to normal as soon as possible so he can relax as he ponders his next move.

8. **Support Him During the Healing Process**- Show your unyielding support for him in this hour. Don't try to avoid him because you feel guilty; be there for him. All the same, don't live in that guilt. Repent to GOD and try to reestablish your relationship with GOD.

9. **Show Regret**- If a man decides to stick around after you've had an affair, it's because he loves you, and he still wants to believe that the marriage will work out. A lot of men walk away; however, because the wife didn't seem to be sorry for her actions. She was so defensive; she became offensive. He has to know that you are sorry, you regret what you did, and that you would never do it again.

10. **Don't Try to Force Sex On Him Right Now**- A lot of women try to hurry up and fix their marriages by offering themselves to their husbands sexually. This ends up

working against the women because many times, sex serves as a reminder to the man as to what these women have done. He'll notice your sounds and movements and suddenly realize that it was not sacred to him. At one point, he thought he was the best lover you'd had, but now, he feels incompetent. Let him pursue you sexually. Don't throw yourself at him trying to rush the problem out the door. Know this: A man can have sex with you and still not plan to stick it out with you. Sex after adultery oftentimes works against the woman and not for her. If he doesn't touch you, don't become angry and emotional. He just doesn't want to hear the sounds audibly because he has now associated those sounds with your affair mentally. Let him recover and let him pursue you.

11. **If He Wants to Be Alone Sometimes to Think, Let Him!** Men like quiet time to think. If he says that he's about to go for a ride, don't try to intervene. Simply tell him that you love him and let him go. Pray for his safety and make sure the house is in order when he returns.

12. **If He Wants a Divorce or Separation, Let Him Go.** A hurt man will likely request a separation or divorce. It's not that he wants it; he just doesn't know what he wants at that moment. He wants to go somewhere else to clear his mind. If you show love, let him know you don't want to separate or divorce, but let him go without a dramatic scene;

he'll likely return home once his mind has been cleared. At the same time, he will see that you are giving him the room he needs to heal, and this will show you in a better light.

13. **Don't Threaten Him or Yourself-** The worst thing you can do is threaten him with divorce, bodily harm, taking his children away, taking his personal belongings away or threatening to harm yourself. Understand that your husband fell in love with a woman who was calm, loving and likely faithful. If you change from being her to becoming an emotional wreck, he will probably file for divorce because he wants no part of the woman that has manifested. Threatening to harm yourself won't show him that you love him; it'll cast you in a "crazy" light.

14. **Be Meek, Humble and Quiet-** A meek, humble and quiet woman is attractive to most men. Don't be loud, abrasive and puffed up.

For every household that adultery occurs in, there may be a different set of rules to recovery that applies. You simply need to know your mate, and if you know him, you will know whether or not to apply any of the tips listed to your marriage.

Recovering from adultery is no easy process, but with the help of GOD, you will manage.

CHAPTER 11

Sleeping With the Enemy
......Literally

One thing about marriage: It is a constant trying of our faith and our patience. Marriage is forgiveness training at the master level. If forgiveness isn't one of your strengths, your marriage will likely pay the ultimate price: divorce.

We are imperfect creatures who have married imperfect creatures and made a perfect mess. In the midst of that mess is the reality of who we married. It takes us years to put together the whole face of the man we've married. Before then, we were still married to that man in our imaginations; the one who has wooed us since we were young women. The first to second year is usually the "drop off" point when we realize that we are building a life with a complete stranger. By years three or four, we have buried the imaginary man and are trying to build a life with the new guy. All the same, the husband realizes that the woman he thought he was getting simply does not exist. At this point in your marriage, the two of you are actually meeting one another for the first time. You are just coming to the realization that you don't really know one another, but you do want to try and make it work out. After all, you've grown accustomed to one another, and you've learned to love each other somewhat.

As a woman, you've probably experience a decline in your physical interest towards your husband. He doesn't care that you aren't who he thought you were; he still enjoys sleeping with you, but you have changed. Sex to you isn't this grand party that you must attend anymore. You love your husband, and your sex life is decent, but you're just not that interested. What happened?

Women are receptors, and men are projectors. Women are the wombs of the earth; we take whatever life the man in our lives gives us, and we make something out of it. Again, we are reflective and will reflect back to the man what he is showing to us. Men don't often store issues; they project them. In a man's mind, he is rarely guilty of any wrong-doing; therefore, he will often project the guilt back onto his wife...who ends up storing the issue. Every issue that you store as a woman, you will birth out in due season. It may come out in the form of an argument; it may come out in the form of a lack in sexual interest towards your spouse. Any issue that has not been dealt with will often ride along with you in your heart during good and bad times. When times are bad, those issues will often rise up against your spouse. At this time, your husband to you is your enemy, and it is hard to sleep with the enemy.

"Be ye angry, and sin not: let not the sun go down upon your wrath: Neither give place to the devil" *(Ephesians 4:26).*

There is a reason that GOD warns us not to let the sun go down on our wrath. The reason is anger is a seed that eventually turns to unforgiveness. It's not a sin to be angry, but unforgiveness is an iniquity. This means it is a condition of the heart. There is a difference between a sin and an iniquity. A sin is an act of rebellion committed against GOD'S WORD. Iniquity is being turned away from GOD in your heart. Iniquity is a heart condition that the person carries around with them every day. An evil heart will not be worn by a holy woman. If the heart is evil, the woman is evil. Anytime we allow the sun to set while we are angry, we give that anger time to root itself. When anger roots itself, it begins to form iniquity in our hearts. As a woman, you know that it can be difficult to release issues of yesterday when they haven't been properly put away by the spouse. But if you don't put them away yourself, the way you feel about your spouse will begin to change. As unforgiveness roots itself, you will find your spouse even less appealing than you did when you were just angry. Sex may go from being good to being decent to being repulsive. Some women never get to the state where they absolutely hate having intercourse with their husbands, but most women get to the state where it's no longer something to write home about. Is it because he sucks in the bedroom? No; it's often because you have some ought against him stored up in your heart. How you feel about him will affect how he feels to you, since women aren't often aroused by their flesh; a woman's mind has to be aroused before her body follows suit.

When you are withholding sex from your husband, you are in the same committing adultery with the enemy. Satan has penetrated your heart and planted all manners of evil in you against your husband. Neither you nor your husband are perfect; that's a given, but you forgot to abort problems that were conceived 300 arguments ago. Now those issues are festering in your marriage. You didn't realize it, but it changed how you saw your husband, and it changed how he saw you. He notices that you often have a bad attitude for no apparent reason, and he has learned to avoid you on those days. Because he doesn't understand, he tries to fix the problem with sex, but you're just not interested. If you do give in, it's obviously just a project to you that needs to be completed so you can get to the next project. This is the sin of iniquity, and you must be delivered from it to move forward.

Your husband is not your enemy; Satan is. The two of you have to learn to stick together against the enemy; otherwise, he will divide you against one another. As a woman and a wife, you will find just how powerful your mind is when simple things begin to affect your sex life.

-CHAPTER 12-

Bedroom Blues

I have listened to a lot of women sing the "bedroom blues." When I was in the world, I was almost afraid of getting married because I'd heard some married women complain about how lousy their husbands were. In the church, I don't hear this as often, but I have heard it. Many married women say their husbands suck in the bedroom.

Bedroom issues are not always the fault of the husband. Oftentimes, the problem is that the wife doesn't communicate to her husband what she likes or dislikes, because women were taught to be sensitive to a man's pride. If the husband asks his wife whether or not she enjoys him, she'd put on a grin and tell him what he wants to hear. This is a huge mistake, because many husbands never get the chance to become better lovers. They are being lied to and then denied, and that's behavior that GOD frowns upon.

What should you do if your husband sucks in the bedroom? Here are a few tips:

1. **Tell him the truth**- If he knows the truth, he will likely try to do better. The issue with many men is that their definition of good sex is not always our definition of good sex. At the same time, a man will often try to sex his wife the same way he sexed the woman he had before her, because the previous woman probably liked certain acts. You have to introduce him to yourself intimately just as you introduced him to your personality. If you tell a man the truth, and he loves you, he'll likely become a real treat.
2. **Make sure the issue is not you**- Sometimes women carry their attitudes into the bedroom. Are you storing any unforgiveness towards him? Or are you expecting this experience to suck like the last few experiences, so you've given up? These are all issues within yourself, and you have to address yourself to change them.
3. **Make sure no one else is in your bedroom**- Sometimes women go into marriages with soul ties from previous relationships still in existence. In these cases, it's not that the husband is a lousy lover; the problem is often that he is not as good as _____(insert name there). If that's the case, you need to seek deliverance from that existing soul tie.
4. **Show him what you like; don't just talk about it**- A man who loves his wife wants to know how to please her, but telling him what to do isn't always enough. Showing

him what you like is always better.

5. **Change your bedroom around**- Sometimes a simple re-arrange of the furniture can set the mood. Cluttered furniture often frustrates the atmosphere in the bedroom. Also make sure that you aren't surrounded by depressing colors like red or black. These colors have been known to cause depression when they are the major color in a room.

6. **Come against your thoughts**- Don't allow negative thoughts to fester in your mind. Come against your way of thinking and introduce your mind to a new way of thinking. Tell yourself that you love and enjoy your husband.

7. **Forgive him**- If he has done anything against you, forgive him. Also remember to forgive him for any bad sexual encounters the two of you had. He's human.

8. **Plan romantic encounters with him at home and away from home**- Don't become monotone with your husband. You can plan a romantic love-filled night with him in the comfort of your own home.

9. **Be spontaneous**- Everything doesn't have to be planned. When you know what to expect, you will lose interest!

10. **Live in the moment**- Oftentimes, you may find yourself thinking of what needs to be done around the house. The kitchen needs cleaning, the children need spanking and the laundry needs putting away. Get that stuff out of your mind and just enjoy your

husband. It is also good to do these things earlier in the day so you can have a free mind later on.

11. **Give him credit for good experiences, and let him cash in those credits sometimes-** There will be times when you will absolutely adore being with your husband, and then there will be times when the sex wasn't so great to you. If he's happy, let that be enough to make you happy. Just don't let this become commonplace.

As a woman, you will find that most of your issues with your husband are stored up in your heart. It's all in how you feel about him; it's not always how good he is in the bedroom. How he treats you will be a major factor in how your body responds to him. That's why it is very important that you discuss every problem that occurs and put it behind you....not in your heart.

CHAPTER 13

Peace Be Still....Even When He Isn't

Every couple argues. Some people are better fighters than others. You will find that some men don't like to argue and will excuse themselves at the sound of you fussing, and some men will try to go toe-to-toe with you. Either way, arguing, to us, is two people disagreeing loudly; to GOD, it is two people opposing HIM loudly.

Understand that there are many things you and your husband can fight about, but many of them aren't that important to you, so you don't fight about them. For example, let's say Cousin Marie comes to visit you, and this is not a problem for you because Cousin Marie is saved, and she is respectful towards the both of you. But Cousin Zania is a no-no. She's your husband's cousin, and she wants to stay at your house when she comes into town. You don't want her there because she is in the world, disrespectful, and she always brings her demons with her. Hubby, on the other hand, feels obligated to let her stay there. So the two of you battle it out. The husband reminds you that he didn't argue about your Cousin Marie when she came, and you remind him that Cousin Marie is a woman of GOD. The night ends with you crying on a tear-soaked pillow, and your husband has left to go for a walk. How could such a small issue that could have been resolved so easily turn into a mountain? It's easy; neither one of you chose to humble yourselves.

Pride is the number-one marriage killer in the earth, because pride roots itself into the heart of its host, and it impersonates wisdom. A person who is prideful sees the argument as a debate in which he or she must win. Their mind is not set on resolution; their mind is set on winning. Even if you show a proud man (or woman) that he's wrong, he will refuse to humble himself because pride is often followed by shame. Proverbs 29:23 reads, *"A man's pride shall bring him low: but honour shall uphold the humble in spirit."* To be brought low means to be humiliated. The words humble and humiliate are words that relate to one another but are different. To be humble means that you have chosen to be lowly and meek. To be humiliated means you were humbled or brought low by something or someone. Of course, it is better to be humble than to be humbled.

Every argument is rooted in pride; it doesn't matter what set it off. *"**Only by pride** cometh contention: but with the well advised is wisdom" (Proverbs 13:10).* There are two languages that we can speak in a marriage. One language is called wisdom, and the other language is called foolishness. To be "foolish" doesn't mean that you are a fool (since a believer cannot be a fool); to be foolish means you are conducting yourself like a fool. *"A fool uttereth all his mind: but a wise man keepeth it in till afterwards" (Proverbs 29:11).* A fool, according to the scriptures, is an unsaved person.

As human beings, we often make mistakes, and we make decisions that lead to future mistakes. Every day is a struggle to get past yourself and learn to wear the wisdom of GOD. It's not easy to be led by the spirit when you are accustomed to being led by your flesh, but you'll manage if you depend on GOD. Because we often follow our flesh's lead, we often trip over consequences and are reminded that we are in no way perfect creatures. This is where arguments come into play. You have two people who are accustomed to being the heads of their own lives, but they are trying to merge their lives together. They are like a two-headed snake; one wants to go in one direction, while the other has his mind made up to go in another direction. Neither of the two is willing to compromise.

As a wife, you are sometimes right, and you are sometimes wrong. But when you're right most of the time, it's easy to become prideful and set your mind to go against your husband out of pride or fear. You believe you make a better leader than he does, because in the game of life, you've got more points than him. So when he comes in with another silly idea or not-so-smart choice, you rage against him because you now see him as a "dummy." This is pride. The only time you will see your husband as "dumb" is when you see yourself as "smart." You may argue and say that this isn't the case with you, but if you see him as "dumb," this is the case with you. The word "dumb" (the way it's used nowadays) means to lack intelligence in comparison to a person or thing. Who are you comparing him to? As women, we know how we want our husbands to be, but we don't know how to get them there. That's because we were never designed to "get them there." We were designed to accompany along the journey.

But let's say that your husband keeps making not-so-smart choices, and you're tired of accompanying him on the red carpet of ignorance. What should you do? First off, you have to remain humble throughout the course of your marriage if you don't want to end up as a divorce statistic. Secondly, you must understand that he is designed to stand; therefore, anytime he falls; he is not bringing you down, he is simply learning to stand.

Imagine a child that's learning to walk. He stands up with his legs trembling, and then he falls down. After he falls, he flips over and gets back up again. He will do this again and again until he learns to stand on his own. As a mother, you wouldn't keep carrying him out of fear that he will fall, because you want him to learn to stand on his own. If he doesn't learn to stand on his own, it could only mean that he's crippled. He has the legs to stand but no knowledge of how to stand. Your husband is the same way! Every choice he makes is either a step towards being the man you've been praying for or a fall. When he falls, you can't come running to criticize or rebuke him. You have to encourage him to stand on his own. You can't keep carrying him, and you can't keep babying him. That is to say that your husband is GOD'S baby, and he is learning to stand on HIS WORD. Anytime he gets in the flesh and acts like a man, he is simply stumbling; but he'll get back up again if you continue to pray for him and believe GOD on his behalf. Sadly enough, many men never learn to stand, because they have a wife who is screaming in their ears every time they trip. That's why you will find that more men walk away from marriages than women do. He wants to stand, but she won't let him. He knows that he will probably never stand with her because she keeps standing against him, so he leaves. This isn't to justify a man abandoning his family, because it's never good to see a home that's been broken up. This is to say that as a wife, we need to be careful that we don't try to over-mother our husbands. To be nurturing is good; to be supportive is great, but to trust GOD with your husband is better.

Maybe someone on his job upset him today, or maybe a family member upset him. Maybe you upset him. What should you do when he's angry and won't sit still?
1. If he's upset with you, apologize, humble yourself and give him his space...even if you're right. You don't always have to audition for the role of the Decision-Making CEO in the marriage by showing him your right-stats. Sometimes, it is better to let him see the truth on his own. After a while, he

will recognize how invaluable you are to the marriage.

2. Don't taunt him. One of the worst things you can do is taunt a pride-filled man, or a man who is hurting. Remain humble and let him process.

3. Call your peace back to you. The worst thing to do with a pride-filled man is to get in the flesh with him. I remember when I used to contend with my husband word-for-word. That was until I discovered the power of silence. Truthfully, I got more by being quiet than I ever did by arguing. Keep your peace and you'll cause him to follow suit.

4. Speak peace over your husband. Remember, you are his help meet (mate), and the two of you are in this together. GOD calls you one person. If the left side of your physical body was sick, would you let it stay sick just because your right side is well? That's how you have to think in marriage. Your husband is your other half. When he's not happy, it's your job to usher peace and joy into the home.

5. Keep it normal. When a husband is out of place, he will often recognize that he is the one in the wrong if everything in the house is still running normally.

6. Do something nice for him. One weapon against unrest and pride is kindness. When my husband would get puffed up and start arguing, I learned to go out and buy something nice for him. I give it to him with love and say, "I love you." This breaks

him every time, because I don't break the mirror that I am to get in the flesh with him. This causes him to see his reflection and realize how simple he's been acting.

7. He's not a dog; don't rub his nose in his mistakes. You will have those occasional moments where you are granted the luxury of being right. At this time, he's humiliated and hoping that it'll all just blow over, but you have to remain humble before he will remain humble. When he's wrong, just move on as if you didn't notice his slip-up. When you are right, you have to glorify GOD by letting your husband learn from his wrong in silence.

8. Don't take it personally, but pay attention to what he says to and of you. When a man is angry, he'll often lash out verbally. Now, he shouldn't be verbally abusive, but sometimes, men say what they really feel about you during their overheating. He may say that you argue too much; he's tired of coming home to the same old thing; you don't keep a clean house; you're beginning to act too much like your mother and so on. Don't let this cut you; let it inform you. Be kind and loving, and take some time to reflect on what he said. This could be a real issue that has been lying dormant in your marriage. Then again, it could be a manipulation attempt, so be sure to pray about what was said...but keep moving forward; don't get stuck in hurt feelings.

9. Let him get the last word. I know this is

hard (I'm a woman too), but it is better to let him release his frustration than it is for the two of you to end up frustrated. It's not about who wins or who loses the argument, because when two people argue, no one wins but GOD.

10. Bind up the devil and any force he may have sent out against your husband, yourself, your children or your marriage. Sometimes, what you are witnessing is your husband folding in the heat of battle. You have a Sword too. Stand with your husband and come against the enemy. Let your husband know that you are for him, not against him.

I know we talked about how to help him stay in a peaceful state of mind, but what about you? What can you do when you are upset?

1. Humble yourself. All too often, the issue isn't with the spouse. The issue is that we are warring with something we need to be warring against: pride. Humble yourself and let GOD fight your battles.

2. Go into another room and pray. Prayer changes things. At the same time, alone time gives you more time to think and clear your head.

3. Cast down all evil imagination and every high thing that exalts itself against the knowledge of GOD. This is scriptural. Go to battle against your mind, and refuse to back down to any desire to fight or pity yourself.

4. Do NOT call your friends or family

members to tell them what is going on in your home. This is an error that pierces the heart of many marriages. Stay calm and give it to GOD.

5. Let GOD be GOD. The issue that arises when we are upset is we want to play GOD, so we try to fix whatever we perceive as broken. When we do this, we end up prolonging the process because GOD will not share HIS glory with you or me. Instead, when you go forward, GOD will often stay put to let you see that you are not HIM.

6. Don't attempt to discuss the issue with your husband when you are upset. The world has it all wrong. Being angry is not the time to discuss a problem. When you're angry, you need to go somewhere and deal with how you feel. When you're calm and happy with one another, then is the time to discuss issues that have been plaguing the marriage. Remember to do it in love and without negative emotions.

7. Go and write him a note. Even though you shouldn't talk to him when you're upset, you will find that writing him a note will be very therapeutic. Tell him how you feel and then destroy the note. This works almost every time.

8. Say the opposite of what you want to say, but do it in love, not sarcasm. Remember, the real issue is how you feel; not whatever made you feel that way. You can deal with the wrongs in a calm manner, but when

you're spinning out of control with anger, you need to deal with that anger. Simply tell him that you love him and excuse yourself from the room. When you leave a man alone with his head, he'll often feel bad about mishandling you.

9. Go for a jog <u>if</u> it's still daylight out, and you're in a safe area. If not, stay at home and exercise. Exercising releases what scientists refer to as "feel good" hormones. Sometimes, taking your mind off the problem and focusing on something else does wonders for your marriage!

10. Take some time to consider what you feel and what he feels. Many times, you will find that he is right and you are wrong. Consider the issue and come up with some solution proposals before approaching your husband.

Remember, peace does not live in a house; peace lives on the inside of you, but pride often evicts it. Never allow pride to rent your heart or discount your marriage.

-CHAPTER 14-

Thinking Like a Queen

There is a way of thinking that would stop divorce right in its tracks. There is a way of thinking that would send the enemy fleeing for cover. That way of thinking is faith thinking.

Most believing women want to be the wife described in Proverbs 31, but there is something we all need to understand about her. It wasn't her works that made her a wife worth bragging on; it was her faith. Every work she did was the result of her faith, and not the other way around. There are many women out who will do the works that a man wants, but their way of thinking will always get in their way eventually. Your way of thinking is either your prison or your castle.

The wife in Proverbs 31 was selfless, not selfish. She was a nurturer, a provider and a wife who brought honor to her husband. People respected him just because of the wife he had. She worked with her hands and not with her mouth; meaning, she didn't just talk about what needed to be done;

she did it. She was a business woman who didn't go out and buy garments and adornments to cover her body. The Bible tells us that she considered a field and bought it. She was an investor, not a spender. She was a busy woman and not a busy-body. She didn't have time for gossip and vain speech. The scripture tells us that she didn't eat the bread of idleness. Of course, we know what an idle woman does: she gossips, thinks too much about the wrong things, engages in adulterous affairs, spends every dollar her husband earns, and brings shame to her husband and children. But the Proverbs 31 wife was too busy providing for her family. When she received a return on the money she'd invested into buying a field, she used it to plant a vineyard. She even made and sold linen garments. She prepared in advance for the storms of life, and she considered the needy.

Nowadays, you'll find many believing women who claim they are a Proverbs 31 wife. But they adorn themselves with costly garments. They gossip, drink and curse any time they are idle. Many open businesses with their mouths, but not with their hands. They talk about what they will do one day, but procrastination is the four walls that keep them boxed in. Most end up working for a company where they complain about their employer and co-workers. When they receive their wages, they don't consider investing the money; they spend it on bills (because they have to) and self (because they want to). Even when they get a lump sum of money, investing is nowhere near their considerations; instead, they spend more money trying to appear to be the wife of a man's dreams, but never actually being her. Many adorn their children with expensive clothing, but their children are hollow inside because Mommy has no wisdom to share with them. They are taught to look their best while being their worst. Some of these mothers neglect their children because there isn't enough money to make Mommy and the children look their Sunday's best; therefore, their children become accustomed to hand-me-downs given to them by concerned family members. Their husbands are hungry for love, hungry for affection, starved of attention and spiritually malnourished. All the while, these unbelieving women go about every day putting in hours working towards the lie that Satan told them. They believe that someday their beauty will pay off; someday, they'll wear the right outfit and get the attention of the right person, and this is going to lead to their greatest payday. They believe the wrong things until their sins hand them a check that they don't have the guts to cash.

To be a wife, you must think like a wife. A wife isn't just a woman that some man married. The term wife is a covenant title given by GOD to a woman who has died to the flesh and been quickened by the Spirit. She is a woman after GOD'S own heart; a woman who was hand-selected by GOD to accompany her husband throughout the course of their lives. She is forgiving, loving, nurturing and understanding. She is a leader, and she is not swayed by the ways of the world; instead, she is a life-altering force that makes change look better than sin to every person who comes in contact with her. Her husband trusts her. He knows that no man has enough strength, beauty or money to sway her, because she isn't grounded by her flesh; she is grounded in her faith. Her children are well-groomed, but more than that, they are filled with the wisdom that Mommy shared with them, and they are proud to call her Mother. They aren't adorned with expensive clothes, but they are clean and well groomed. Their Mother saves of her increase to provide a better future for them, not a better outfit. Other children are drawn to her because they want her to be their Mother.

A GOD-ordained wife is always sowing good seeds today so that her family can harvest them tomorrow. Even when she leaves the earth, her name and legacy continues to live on. Even the hoodlums loved and respected her, because she was known inside and outside of her community as a woman after GOD'S own heart. Her daughters grow up to pattern after her; her sons grow up and search the heart of GOD to find a wife just like her. Her husband never forgets to thank GOD for her. She is his crown, and her smile is the sparkle that lights every day he spends with her. He works hard to provide for her and his children with her, because a woman like that deserves nothing but the best. Even if he lost his job today, he would go out and cut grass, rake leaves, paint walls or do whatever he has to do to make sure that she is well taken care of. If he can't provide for her properly, there is no need to worry; he will eventually find his footing in success because he won't rest until he can give her the world. When he is down and out, she is there to lift him up. She encourages him, and she makes him want to be a man even better than the man he is. Even when age has stolen her beauty, she is still the most beautiful woman he has ever seen because he sees her heart, and it radiates through her. Even when she leaves the earth, her family grieves, but they rest in knowing that she is in eternity with the Most High GOD. This encourages each and every one of her children, and others that knew her, to live a life worthy of honor by GOD.

Most women want to be a Proverbs 31 wife, but you have to have the mindset of a queen to sit on a throne worthy of mentioning in the Bible. How do you get the mindset of a queen?

1. Recognize that you are your husband's crown. Even though a crown sits atop the king's head, it is not his head or authority figure. A crown simply makes him look good and lets everyone know that he is royalty. Don't be a crown of thorns to him.

2. Because your husband found you, he is favored by GOD, but you can end up being the very tool Satan uses to cut his phone line to heaven. If you keep getting in the flesh with him, he'll keep coming in the flesh trying to cover you, because a husband was designed by GOD to cover his wife.
   "Likewise, ye husbands, dwell with them according to knowledge, giving honour unto the wife, as unto the weaker vessel, and as being heirs together of the grace of life; that your prayers be not hindered" (1 Peter 3:7).

3. Queen Vashti was called, but she did not

come forward. Queen Esther was chosen, and she came forward when she wasn't even called. Queen Vashti was rebellious and ended up losing her crown, but Queen Esther was obedient and ended up wearing a glorious crown that would be talked about for centuries to come.

4. A queen doesn't lose her crown when the heat is turned up; she establishes it.

5. In order to be a queen, you must know the King of Kings. It's not enough just to know that HIS Name is JESUS; you need to have an intimate relationship with HIM where HE knows your voice because of the countless prayers you send up daily, and you know HIS.

6. An argument is not enough to remove a queen from her throne; you're going to need security, and lots of it.

7. A queen continually works towards a better kingdom, even when the one she is living in is great.

8. A queen will take a shack and make a castle out of it. She will take a house and make it home. Always remember that peace in a home normally comes with the wife and because of the wife.

9. A queen will never share the affairs of her marriage with others; instead, she takes them to the king of the castle, and if he doesn't handle them properly, she takes them to the King of Kings. She knows order, and she refuses to let disorder rule her home.

10. A queen will fish for wisdom and feed it to

her family.

There was another queen in the Bible that I'm sure not many women want to pattern after. She was Queen Jezebel. Jezebel was a Phoenician woman; the daughter of a king. King Ahab, who was the King of North Israel, married her against GOD'S orders. Queen Jezebel was a worshipper of Baal. Baal worship is pretty much the worship of flesh.

When Jezebel became queen of North Israel, she did not sit on her husband's right hand side; she sat on his left; meaning, she took his place. Jezebel emasculated her husband and ruled the kingdom that was handed to him by GOD. She killed the prophets of GOD and sent out letters in Ahab's name without Ahab's consent. Jezebel severed Ahab's relationship with GOD for eternity!

There are so many characteristics to that wicked Jezebel that are common in today's woman. Many wives nowadays have adopted the women's empowerment movement; a movement started by Jezebel herself. Of course, many women don't go out and march, but their speech and lifestyle bears witness to what they believe. Women seduced or inhabited by a Jezebel spirit say things like:

- I don't need a man. I can do it all on my own.
- I don't need a man; just give me two AA batteries, and I'm good.
- My husband knows who's boss!
- My husband has my last name.
- When I get a husband, he's going to have my

last name.
- I wear the pants in my house.
- What about me?

That's because not much is taught about the Jezebel spirit, nor are many women being taught the importance of staying covered by their husbands. Of course, this has a lot to do with the fact that there are many men out there who abuse their roles as heads of the households. Needless to say, these men are not men of GOD, even if they are masquerading as such. That is to say that many women are distracted by titles and lies to the point where they've started responding by liberating themselves. A man needs a woman, just as a woman needs a man. Two women cannot produce children together because they are both receptors, just as two television sets cannot empower one another to come on. A television set has to be plugged into an electrical outlet in order to work properly. It is then and only then that the television set can pick up signals from neighboring towers. As women, we are the same way. We have to be with a man to produce children. This is the only way we'll receive signals from GOD to carry those children to term. All the same, two men cannot produce children together because they are both projectors.

Here are a few things about Jezebel that you should know so you can avoid channeling her ways or even that spirit:

1. Jezebel was queen, but she acted as king. Jezebel did not submit to Ahab; Ahab submitted to Jezebel. He even took on her

religion.

2. Jezebel was a worshipper of the flesh. Oftentimes, your flesh will wake up and make its demands. In those times, you will want to give in, and you will want your husband to give in to the desires of your flesh. Stop it! Come against your flesh every time you realize it is rising up.

3. Ahab wasn't given permission by GOD to marry Jezebel. He was warned against it! You may not be the wife GOD chose for your husband; then again, you may be her. If you are not the wife GOD designed for him, you will have a great struggle ahead of you as you attempt to work together with the tools you have, but you have to understand that these are not the tools he needs. Repent and ask GOD to re-assign you to him since you are married to him, and to give you the tools to aid him along in his assignment.

4. Jezebel was a liar who used people as tools. She surrounded herself with all sorts of people that she used at her convenience. When Naboth would not give Ahab his inheritance, she held a feast and had two scoundrels seated on each side of Naboth. Each scoundrel did as he was told; he lied on Naboth.

5. Jezebel hated true prophets, but she loved false prophets. If a true prophet bothers you, but you love prophets who tickle your flesh, you need to seek the face of GOD for deliverance.

To become the wife GOD has designed you to be, you need CHRIST-like thinking. What you believe will change your posture. If you believe you are just another woman who is waiting for a man to claim her, you will carry yourself as such, and you will see men as potential husbands. If you believe you are a wife in waiting, and that your ONE and ONLY husband is coming, you will see men as men. You won't try to guess outside of GOD who is who for your life. If you are married already and you believe you were given to your husband by GOD, you will carry yourself like a treasure. Your confidence will radiate through your faith, and your love will prove to be invaluable. If you believe that you married the wrong man, you will carry yourself like a victim, and your regrets will darken your countenance. You will see him as a temporary fixture, and the "man of your dreams" will still be in your head whispering sweet nothings to you. Yes, you will be in an adulterous affair with your imagination. Because you didn't cast the thought down, you're willing to cast your husband away.

Pay attention to your posture; it speaks volumes of what you believe. When you stand on your faith, you will stand up straight, and sit upright. Even if you married the wrong man, it's not all his fault; it's yours too. But the two of you have to glorify GOD with your marriage by showing the world that GOD can take a mistake and make it look like and be a blessing. Sure, when you marry the wrong man, you will go through some trials and tribulations as the foundation of your marriage (which likely was flesh) is torn down, and you are united as one in

CHRIST JESUS. You can survive this ordeal when you realize that GOD loves you so much that HE wants to establish your marriage in HIM. As a wife after GOD'S own heart, your words won't be abrasive to your husband; they will be soothing, encouraging, and words designed to bless him. Even if he isn't the right man today, your chaste behavior will ensure that the devil can't stick around him too much longer.

A crown doesn't just sit on a man's head; it bears witness to what kind of king he is. It also influences his decisions. For example, do you think a man who is wearing a crown too tight for him will think to walk in his garden to smell the roses? His first thought is to get that crown off his head. All the same, do you think a man wearing a crown of thorns will think to take you on a date? No way. He's going to think of a way to carefully remove that crown so that he doesn't get hurt any more than he has to. Do you think a man wearing a crown that is too big for him can extend his scepter when his queen needs to speak to him? No. He'll extend his scepter to every female who approaches him, because the crown he has doesn't fit him properly and keeps covering his eyes. But a man wearing a beautiful and valuable crown will take good care of his crown. It's not too heavy for him, but it's weighty enough to let him know that it's there. He polishes it with words, and he wants to show it off to everyone. A king never leaves his castle without his queen. Even if he leaves you at home, he carries you with him in his heart.

We want the man after GOD'S heart; we want the man who could love us beyond our greatest imaginations, but how many of us are willing to be the queen that man wants? If you let GOD change your mind, HE will in return change your husband's mind because your husband has to meet and cover you where you are. One thing you will notice about a man is that he will be as respectable as the wife he covers or as detestable as the woman he uncovered. Whatever you decide you want in a husband, you must first learn to be that in a wife. Study and show yourself approved, and you will not only become that Proverbs 31 wife that everyone talks about, but you will become a platform for your husband to become better than the "man of your dreams."

www.ingramcontent.com/pod-product-compliance
Lightning Source LLC
Chambersburg PA
CBHW070105070426
42448CB00038B/1727